ETHICS PROTOCOLS AND RESEARCH ETHICS COMMITTEES
SUCCESSFULLY OBTAINING APPROVAL FOR YOUR ACADEMIC RESEARCH

Dan Remenyi
Nicola Swan
Ben Van Den Assem

ETHICS PROTOCOLS AND RESEARCH ETHICS COMMITTEES
SUCCESSFULLY OBTAINING APPROVAL FOR YOUR ACADEMIC RESEARCH Copyright © The authors

First published June 2011 by
Academic Publishing International Ltd, Reading, UK
info@academic-publishing.org

ISBN: 978-1-906638-99-3

Printed in the UK by Good News Digital Books

Contents

Preface

This book addresses Ethics Protocols related to Masters, Doctoral and other Research which will be conducted under the auspices of a university or similar institution.

Conducting academic research to the highest ethical standards is essential for both the researcher personally and the university or institution at which he or she is working. If the highest standards of ethical behaviour are not maintained then the researcher and the university or institution can easily fall into disrepute.

In recent years it has become more challenging to conduct quality academic research. There are several reasons for this, one of which is the need to have Ethics Protocol approval before the research can begin.

The issue of ethics is ubiquitous in academic research. Some universities claim that all research raises ethical issues, although it is difficult to see how such a blanket claim could be correct. University codes of ethics can be extensive, addressing issues such as what should be and should not be researched; how the research should be conducted; how researchers should work with each other; how the research should be written up, to mention only a few issues.

Universities have become more conscious of ethical issues and more concerned about their responsibilities in this respect. To this end numerous Research Ethics Committees (RECs) and research ethics policies and procedures have been set up.

Although each university has its own procedures with respect to Ethic Committees and how a researcher can obtain ethics approval for his or her research, they generally follow the same basic principles.

This book discusses the background to the need for Ethic Protocols and Ethic Committees and describes the way permission is obtained and provides useful advice about how to cope with the Ethics Protocol approval process.

It is important to note that there is much more to the subject of academic ethics than is addressed in this book. There are many sources of advice about how research should be conducted in the most ethical fashion. This book provides advice in dealing with the REC which increasingly research students and degree candidates need to address. It is also important to bear in mind that outside of the medical faculties, the need for ethics approval is relatively new for universities and that universities are in the process of finding their way through what is a complex set of issues.

Acknowledgements

A book such as this cannot be written without the help and assistance of many staff and research candidates who have brought to us examples of their experiences with RECs. These people have been from several different universities in this country and abroad. Although we have not been able to repeat all their stories here we would like to acknowledge that these people have made a contribution to our current thinking with regards to Ethic Committee and Ethics Protocol approval.

We would also like to acknowledge a number of friends who have read drafts of the text and offered helpful advice concerning the content and the tone with which the book was being written.

How to use this book

This book has been written as a guide to researchers who have to obtain approval for an Ethics Protocol. The book will also be useful to members of university faculties who are involved in advising students about obtaining ethics approval. This is not a 'how-to' book but rather one which provides useful background information. As such it is not intended that every reader will begin at the front and read to the end.

Some readers may wish to go directly to the Chapter 4 on how to complete an ethics application or to Chapter 11 which discusses substantial and non-substantial amendments etc.

Readers who find they need to amend their application for ethics approval should read Chapter 5 first.

Other Chapters provide a background and explain in a more general way how RECs and Ethics Protocols work.

Copies of some of the documentation required by a REC are supplied in the Appendices. These should not be used by readers and are supplied for illustrative purposes only. Each university has its own instruction pages and forms and these should be acquired by a researcher for his or her use in obtaining an Ethics Protocol approval.

There are different ways of describing the individuals with whom a researcher comes into contact and or/who contribute during the course of a research project. Names such as respondent, informant, participant or subject are commonly used. It has been decided not to standardise on one name in this book, but to use different names in different parts of the book, reflecting the preferences of the three authors.

A blog has been created for those who would like to contribute to the discussion on this topic. See http://ethics-dilemmas.blogspot.com/

searcher needs to have sufficient strength to control temptations[1] such as this.

Academic research can require researchers to work with people who have intense feelings about the subject being studied. For example, a study into how organisations handle redundancies would most probably require the researcher to interview people who had been made redundant. Being made redundant can be a traumatic event in the life of an individual and an interview on this subject would need to be handled with considerable care. If the informant were to give an indication of not coping well with such an interview, for example if the informant began crying, then it would behove the researcher to suggest that the interview be terminated until the informant felt better. The interview could be rescheduled for the next day or the next week. It would be improper for the researcher to try to press on with an interview if the informant was emotionally upset. This is of course no more than common sense.

The issue of researcher integrity is challenging. In the first place it is difficult to define this word. Most people would agree that integrity means more than just being correct or following the rules, i.e. being honest, or even having the best interests of others in mind. One understanding of the word suggests that integrity is about having the will to be fair, and following it through with actions. It implies being honest, not just with other people with whom one comes into contact, but also with oneself. Shakespeare expressed this succinctly when he wrote in Hamlet Act 1, scene 3, 78–82

> to thine own self be true,
> And it must follow, as the night the day,
> Thou canst not then be false to any man.

This level of honesty is more than many people can cope with. Integrity implies a state of wholeness and self confidence in the personality of the individual.

---

[1] The main temptation here is that researchers can sometimes earn a substantial amount of money by teaching on undergraduate programmes. Another temptation is to become involved with other university work for the prestige which can accompany working for a university.

An individual's integrity is challenged continuously as he or she interacts with others in society. This is because there are different versions of what integrity means and there are different ways of interpreting the normal course of everyday events. People will have different points of view about the same issue. It is probably not possible to find a large number of people who would completely agree in all respects with any given definition of integrity or any one interpretation of the integrity of an event.

Although we talk about academic research being supervised, much of the work actually happens with the researcher on his or her own with little or no interference or guidance from the supervisor. It is because of this freedom that it is important to discuss early on in the research process the ethics rules with which the researcher needs to comply.

One of the reasons why a research Ethics Protocol is so important is that it makes researchers aware of the need for integrity and for transparency in the research process. For those who are already familiar with this requirement the research protocol is a reminder. The application for research permission and the approval of the Ethics Protocol may be seen as a promise made by the researcher to conduct the research with the highest level of integrity.

A promise is only a promise

But it has to be understood that no matter how clearly the ethics rules are spelt out and no matter how enthusiastically the researcher embraces these rules, at the end of the day the only thing that matters is how the researcher conducts him or herself. A promise is always nothing more than a statement about what might happen in the future and we hope that the events which will take place will be influenced by the promise[2]. It is on this basis that a REC should consider Ethics Protocol applications.

---

[2] It has been said that if a promise has not been kept it was not a promise in the first place. Readers may take their own position on this philosophical point.

Assumptions

From the above it can be seen that academic research operates under several different sets of assumptions. It is first assumed that the researcher has the intellectual, physical and emotional strengths to complete the degree. These are difficult to assess from an ex ante point of view and that is why the completion rates of research degrees are often poor. Maybe universities could spend more time and effort exploring how these issues could be assessed and understood before anyone is accepted for a research degree.

Secondly, it is assumed that the researcher will be adequately mature, sensitive and committed to working with integrity throughout the research.

There is no easy way of assessing an individual's maturity, sensitivity and integrity. There is also the fact that a research degree is a voyage of discovery and the views of an academic researcher are likely to change during the period of the degree. It is not possible to be sure that these changes will all be for the better.

The Ethics Protocol and the Research Ethics Committee

It is not argued here that because these issues are so challenging nothing should be done about research integrity. Of course a prospective researcher should apply for permission and a REC should carefully inspect the research plans and make appropriate recommendations where appropriate. However, it is not in this process or the documents created during the execution of this process that the integrity of the research and the researcher lie and it is important to be aware of this. The Woody Allen comment in the film Annie Hall, quoted above, reminds us of the fact that it is probably impossible to look deeply enough into a person's psyche to be able to assess his or her integrity.

Chapter 1

Ethics Protocols – The Key Issues

"Even when the experts all agree, they may well be wrong."

Bertrand Russell cited in Peter, L.J. The Peter Prescription: How to Make Things Go Right, Bantam, NY, 1972.

1.1 What is this thing called ethics?

Ethics is a branch of philosophy which addresses issues of human conduct related to a sense of what is right and what is wrong and as such it may be regarded as a society's code of moral conduct. It is closely related to the idea of mores, which also refer to that which a society considers to be acceptable and not acceptable behaviour. The ethics and mores of a society are based on the values which the society espouses.

Ethics is situation related and may differ both in terms of location and time. What is ethical among people in one part of the world may not be ethical in another and what was ethical in the year 1000 CE may no longer be the case. It is often influenced by religious and political beliefs of the people concerned. Ethical concerns extend to human choices affecting actions as well as motives and objectives. Humans as a whole or even in groups such as clubs or neighbourhoods do not have a common sense of what is and is not ethical.

Ethics has been a human concern from ancient times with early writers on the subject including Plato and Aristotle. Despite this length of interest, the subject is still one of controversy. There are those who argue that an individual's ethical sense is related to their personality. The behaviour with which an extrovert is comfortable is different to that with which an introvert is comfortable. However, many if not all social groups do impose some sort of ethical stance on its members.

A society's ethical stance can be understood by considering its laws, its customs and how these are put into practice or enforced. An examina-

1

tion of what a society purports to do in terms of its laws and customs can be quite different to what actually happens, which can only be studied by the observation of conduct. There are often gaps between what a society asserts are its values, morals or ethical code and what actually happens in that society. In a similar way there is often a disparity between what people claim as their ethical beliefs and what they actually do. Wittgenstein made this point elegantly when he said, *"Do not ask a man if he is religious. Observe him"*. This type of disparity exists not only at the individual people level but also at the institutional and societal level. In modern times the Declaration of Independence of the United States of America proclaimed that *"All men are born equal"* although at that time slavery was practiced, where men, women and children were being bought and sold in the same fashion as animal livestock.

Changes in ethics can be dramatic over time. Slavery was acceptable not only to the ancient Greeks but also to virtually all of human kind until the 19th century[3]. Ethnic cleansing was practiced by all European countries when they colonised lands in faraway places[4]. Until the 19th century education was generally rationed. With few exceptions there was access to education only for the rich and powerful or those wishing to qualify for a religious position. Government existed to protect the upper class from the rest of society. Diseases and other health related issues were a matter of private concern as access to medical services was not available to the general public. Until modern times there was little concept of freedom of speech. The charges against Socrates were based on the fact that his teachings were corrupting the youth of Athens.

In many respects all this has changed in 21st century Europe. The ethical stance of our society has been described as a caring society in which consideration is given to individuals and their requirements in order to have a life in which they can fulfil their personal potential. This means inter alia access to medical services, education, and other resources required for fulfilling this potential. Specific issues which 21st century

---

[3] Although slavery has been outlawed in most countries it is still practiced in some parts of the world. It is now often referred to as human trafficking. It has been estimated that there may be as many as 20 million people living under slave type conditions.
[4] Although much less common, ethnic cleansing is still practiced in certain parts of the world. It is closely associated with genocide.

Europeans generally recognise are, importance of freedom of movement i.e. to travel at will, freedom of speech, the rule of law and the rights of individuals to privacy. Also recognised as important is the dignity of the individual, courteous behaviour, equity, honesty, fairness, the right to own property and to employ resources for one's own private enrichment.

Of course, there are gaps between what our society aspires to and what happens to individuals. The quality of medical services varies considerably. In general if one can pay for medical services the better they are. The quality of education is a function of the money which is spent on it. Equity before the law can be affected by the amount of fees which are paid to the best lawyers. Freedom of speech has been impacted due to wars which are being pursued. We are tolerant of misleading advertisements which can border on lying. We accept that entrepreneurs from privileged positions accumulate wealth beyond any reasonable amount. We see grinding poverty in almost every society and we permit it to continue. It is no doubt an imperfect world in which we live.

1.2   Society as a patchwork of ethics issues

Ethics applies to different aspects of society. Thus there are ethical issues related to government funding, to airline pricing, telephone hacking or tapping, carbon footprints, sweatshops, to medical treatment and to police behaviour at political protests, to mention only a few areas of concern. To the extent that it is possible to use different lenses through which to see life and society, there are corresponding sets of ethics issues.

1.3   Ethics and academe

Academe is a field of activity in which there are many ethical concerns. These relate to what is taught, how it is taught, what facilities are offered to students, how academics view their responsibility to students and to other faculty members. There are questions related to matters such as objective and timely feedback to students and more personal matters such as bullying and favouritism, to mention only a few issues. It is said that the Internet has facilitated an increased level of plagiarism. This has resulted in the production of various software packages to detect infringements of this type in academic work. There also appears to be a thriving industry built around the demand from students to have

3

essays, projects and even dissertations written for them by ghost writers.

This book is confined to considering issues related to academic research. Specifically it focuses on how researchers can handle their application for the approval of an Ethics Protocol.

1.4   Ethics for academic research

Conducting academic research to the highest ethical standards is essential for both the researcher personally and the university or institution at which he or she is working. If the highest standards are not maintained then the reputation of the researcher and the university or institution could be compromised.

From a high level perspective, ethical concerns in academic research include but are not limited to:-

- The nature of the research question;
- The means by which the research question will be answered;
- The safety and wellbeing of the researcher and all those with whom he or she comes into contact including informants;
- The necessity for the researcher to be open and honest with all those involved with the research;
- The importance of the researcher not misusing the ideas or works of others;
- The application to which the results of the research will be put.

1.4.1   The nature of the research question

In business and management studies there are relatively few research questions which could be intrinsically considered unethical. However, questions related to how to find optimal approaches to defraud individuals would clearly be unsuitable in an academic institution. Exploring how to increase the market size for narcotics would not be acceptable. Even studies on how to encourage a greater use of tobacco or alcohol would not be welcomed.

1.4.2   The means by which the research question will be answered

Ethics Committees focus a considerable amount of their attention on this issue which is central in all Ethics Protocols. The researcher will need to have considered and outlined in some detail the methods that will be used to collect data and will have to understand how these methods can sometimes infringe upon ethics guidelines.

1.4.3   The safety and wellbeing of the researcher and all those with whom he or she comes into contact including informants

The researcher would be expected to ensure, to the best of his or her ability, the safety and well-being of informants. Although researchers' safety is not always explicitly addressed, it is always an important issue. Furthermore, universities now require researchers to apply for permission when it is their intention to work abroad and this may be seen as relating to the safety issue. Recently an application to research the question of money laundering was turned down because the REC believed that to obtain authentic data on this subject the researcher would have to make contact with criminals. This could have resulted in some future danger to the researcher and potentially others, such as the researcher's supervisor.

1.4.4   The necessity for the researcher to be honest with all those involved with the research

Honesty is the central platform on which all academic research needs to be conducted. It is fundamental that the institution trusts the researcher to accurately and fairly report all the activities associated with the research.

1.4.5   The importance of the researcher not misusing the ideas or works of others

There are several ways in which a researcher could misuse the ideas of others. The most common of these is plagiarism and all academic researchers have been subjected to regular awareness programs in this respect.

1.4.6 *The application to which the results of the research will be put*

The application to which the results of the research will be put may not always be evident from the outset. Nonetheless researchers are expected to be aware of this issue and to try to avoid exploring issues which could be used negatively in society.

In Chapter 3 we describe how academe has slowly become aware of the issues related to research ethics over the past 100 years or so. It will also be pointed out that this concern has sprung from the growing realisation that medical researchers have sometimes treated people with callous indifference in the name of research. This type of behaviour was justified by the researcher's belief that he or she was adding something to the body of knowledge which was important to human kind in general.

The university's sensitivity to these issues is at least in part based on the fact that a researcher acquires a significant amount of status in the public's eyes by being able to say that he or she is researching at the university. If the researcher then behaves inappropriately he or she will bring the good name of the university into disrepute.

The Ethics Protocol which has to be approved by a REC is the way academe has chosen to express its concerns about the ethics of research. Universities have based their approval procedures on the medical model of research ethics and this model is now spreading into all Faculties, Schools and Departments.

1.5 What is a Research Ethics Committee?

A REC is a group of individuals who have been charged with ensuring that university research complies with the appropriate standards of ethical behaviour and concerns. An REC performs an oversight function whereby the risks of any inappropriate behaviour on the part of the researcher or researchers is considered. The Committee may refuse permission to proceed with the research or impose restrictions as to how the research may be conducted. A REC which discovers unapproved research may require the researcher to discontinue the research. On the other hand, having examined what the researcher is doing, a REC may grant permission to proceed[5]. The decisions of a REC can normally be challenged through an appeal process.

Many universities will have a number of different levels of RECs ranging from university-wide to departmental Committees.

1.5.1 A university level REC

The academic authority within a university is normally vested in a body called the University Senate and it is the Senate that tends to appoint a university level research REC.[6] The university level REC is charged with ensuring that all research activities within the university, and activities outside the university which include any university involvement and/or which involves humans and/or animals, are conducted in the most ethical way possible. The primary ethical consideration is that no one involved with the research should come to any harm as a result of the research activities being carried out[7]. In some universities this means that all activities which have any research component dealing with humans and animals has to seek approval from the university authorities[8]. In some cases this concern extends down to undergraduate research to cover all activities which are called research and in which there is any element of human or animal involvement. In other universities the focus on ethics is more limited. Some universities are only concerned with ethics at postgraduate level and some universities require the research to intrude on animal or humans in some direct way[9] before the REC becomes involved.

A university level REC will be composed of senior academics and experts in the field of research ethics. There will often be representatives from the medical profession and other outside bodies who have concerns

---

[5] Some universities make a point of asserting that no research project will be granted approval retrospectively. However, in most cases this will depend on exactly what sort of research is involved and the actual level of risk which the university is facing.

[6] This is often a subcommittee of the University Senate.

[7] This includes the researchers themselves.

[8] Other bodies outside of the university which have an interest may also need to authorise the research.

[9] There are of course differences in opinion concerning the definition of the term "direct way".

about the proper conduct of research. There is sometimes a student representative on this Committee. If the researcher seeking approval for his or her research is a member of the REC they will in the normal course of events have to recuse themselves from the decision related to their own proposal.

As will be seen later in this book, because of misconduct of some researchers in the medical field and the pressure from animal rights groups,[10] universities have to take research misconduct seriously. Some universities use the widest possible definition of research as having human contact and now an interview and even the completion of a questionnaire can be thought of as a researcher having human contact which has to be monitored.

Reviewing an applications for a research Ethics Protocol to establish if it is worthy of approval is a time consuming business. As a result the university level REC often delegates the inspection of proposals and protocols to Faculty, School or even Departmental RECs. In some cases the ethics approval has been further delegated and is now vested in the hands of the research supervisor.

1.5.2 A Faculty, School or Departmental REC

The number of applications for Ethics Protocols which a busy university level REC needs to inspect and authorise is substantial and this high level Committee will typically delegate some of this authority to Faculties, Schools or Departments. This is increasingly common as more and more research is being demanded of academics and research has become an increasingly important part of many academic degrees. University level RECs tend to be large as they want to include all the expertise they need but large Committees tend to be cumbersome. In many cases the university level REC will have its own subcommittees which will consider applications before they are presented to the main Committee.

There may be a problem when the Ethics Protocol approval authority is delegated to Faculties, School or Departments. Whereas the university level Committee tends to have access to experts in the field of research

---

[10] It is beyond the scope of this book to explore the issue of animal rights but for those who are interested there are a substantial number of animal rights groups and a considerable number of these can be accessed on the web.

ethics, these other university bodies may not necessarily. In some cases these Committees are populated with academics who have been seconded to the Committee and thus have not much experience of the issues involved in ensuring that research is conducted in an ethical way. This can result in delays and rejections of perfectly adequate arrangements for research projects from an ethics point of view. This can have a negative impact on the morale of the researchers involved and also brings the ethics initiatives of the university into question.

This is hopefully a temporary phenomenon as Faculties, Schools and Departments build up some experience and competence.

1.5.3   *The supervisor as the REC*

In some universities where there are large numbers of students the responsibility to ensure that the research students have a proper Ethics Protocol as well as the function of giving ethics approval has been delegated even further to the supervisor. There are not many supervisors who can claim anything other than a superficial knowledge of the issues involved with research ethics. Having supervisors sign off Ethics Protocols imposes a substantial burden and potentially a risk on the supervisor and is likely to lead to disagreements with research students. In some cases supervisors have simply had students complete an Ethics Protocol form on a "tick" and "flick" basis.

A "tick" and "flick" basis implies that the university has created forms (these look much like questionnaires) which the research student has to fill out. When the form is completed, mostly by ticking boxes , and the supervisor has ensured that all the points of concern have been addressed, the ethics obligation is said to have been attended to. This delegation of ethics responsibility exposes the university, the student and the supervisor to the risk of some future difficulty if a research participant were to complain about any aspect of the research.

1.5.4   *Chairperson's action*

In some situations if a research project does not have significant ethical implications, an Ethics Protocol may be approved by Chairperson's Action. This means that the Chairperson takes the initiative and approves the research programme on his or her own. This is normally subject to the Ethics Protocol application receiving subsequent approval from the

Committee. This procedure of Chairperson's Action suggests that the Chairperson should have considerable knowledge and experience of ethics issues within the research domain.

1.6   What is an Ethics Protocol?

RECs operate by requiring academic researchers to submit an application for the approval of an Ethics Protocol. In order to consider if a proposed research project will comply with the ethics standards required by the university, the researcher will normally have to complete a detailed form which will explain, inter alia, the nature of the research and how it will be conducted. This form will be accompanied by a Participant's Information Document which will be offered to any informants who may be invited to supply data to the research. An example of such a document is provided in Appendix 1. In addition a copy of any proposed measuring instrument such as a questionnaire or an interview schedule will be required by the Committee. Finally a copy of any correspondence which the researcher proposes to undertake with the informants together with a draft Letter of Informed Consent will be required. An example is shown in Appendix 2. RECs can ask for further information and may also require changes to these documents. When the REC is fully satisfied a letter of approval will be given to the researcher. This letter with copies of the various documents described above is referred to as the Ethics Protocol.

The Ethics Protocol is of importance to the researcher for a number of reasons including the fact that it affords protection to the researcher in the event of something going wrong with the research procedures. Provided the researcher has complied with the ethics protocol no blame should accrue to him or her.

The actual procedures involved in obtaining an Ethics Protocol will differ from one university to another and will even differ from one Faculty or School to another. It is important that researchers determine exactly what is required of them in respect of the Ethics Protocol and that they closely follow the instructions.

1.7   When a university Ethics Protocol may not be enough

Collaborative research with individuals from other institutions requires additional ethics approval from the other institution.

Furthermore, research involving any aspect of the health system will need special approval. In the UK it will have to be approved by the relevant committee in the National Health Service and other Health and Social Care organisations. In other countries it will usually require similar approval.

If the researcher or a member of the research team is registered with a professional body he or she may need approval from that body. Even if formal approval is not required the researcher still should comply with the guidelines of his or her professional body[11].

Funding bodies may also require the researcher to obtain ethical clearance from them directly.

On occasions some universities will waive the need to go to the REC if a relevant national body has already given the research its approval.

Research which involves individual adults who are regarded as potentially vulnerable may require additional authorisation before it is begun. According to a UK County Council website:

> *a vulnerable adult is a person aged 18 years or over who is or may be in need of community care services by reason of mental or other disability[12], age or illness and who is or may be unable to take care of him or herself, or unable to protect him or herself against significant harm or exploitation[13].*

---

[11] The Statement of Ethical practice for the British Sociological Association provides useful guidelines. See
http://www.britsoc.co.uk/equality/Statement+Ethical+Practice.htm#_rel
[12] People who are blind, deaf or wheelchair bound fall into this category.
[13] http://www.surreycc.gov.uk/sccwebsite/sccwspages.nsf/Lookup WebPages-ByTITLE_RTF/Definition+of+a+vulnerable+adult?opendocument

by faculty members or by research students and the only consideration was the viability of the project in terms of its academic value. Under these circumstances the major issues were to find, from the literature or in some cases from knowledgeable informants, a suitable research question together with a clear research design. In order to achieve this, researchers often engaged in conversation with a range of individuals in both formal and informal situations. Not infrequently the formal conversations amounted to interviews. In terms of the current attitude towards Ethics Protocols academic researchers are forbidden to interview anyone before ethics approval is acquired. But it may be impossible to settle on a suitable research question and design without detailed conversations/interviews. There is a Catch 22 inherent in this situation[17]. Some researchers would argue that every research project has to have a starting point and that any conversations or interviews held before the starting point is reached is out of the range of interest of the Ethic Committee. There is no universal agreement on this and thus researchers should be careful with regards to any pre-research discussions that are held.

Another issue relating to the keeping of data when conducting case study research, is that of publishing data concerning the organisations which have been visited to acquire data for the study. Case study researchers traditionally include a synopsis of the data obtained from interviews and other sources in their dissertations. Even if the case descriptions are anonymised, readers of the case study might guess which organisation is being described. This led to the conclusion that anonymisation is a challenging matter and sometimes the names of individuals and organisations cannot be adequately anonymised to such an extent that a determined individual cannot discover the name of the person or the organisation.

Requiring an interview schedule to be approved by the REC before use can undermine the need for both flexibility and learning during research activities. Having conducted a few interviews the academic researcher may well wish to modify the interview schedule as a result of what he or she has learnt. Once modified it is not the same interview schedule

---

[17] Some researchers recognise that there may be a need for a pre-research interview which will help validate the importance of the research idea before any formal research begins. In terms of the current attitude towards research protocols it is important not to refer to such conversations as research interviews.

which has been approved by the Ethics Protocol. In qualitative research it is expected that the researcher will respond to the lessons he or she is learning during the research process. More is said about this issue of changes to the Ethics Protocol in Chapter 5 – Amending the Ethics Protocol.

There are problems with regards to the anonymisation of data received by the researcher. Generally speaking Ethics Protocols require data to be anonymised soon after it has been collected by the researcher. At the same time informants are permitted to contact researchers and inform them that they wish to withdraw from the research and have their data removed at any time. If after a period of a number of weeks and given that the data will have been anonymised, how will it be possible for the researcher to locate the specific data and remove it from the database? It is suggested that informants should be advised that after a certain number of days of the data being supplied, say for example, seven, it will have been anonymised and therefore it will not be possible to determine which record in the database belongs to any particular person.

In quantitative research a researcher may have specified the type of analysis which he or she intends to use. After examining some of the actual data collected it is possible that the researcher may wish to employ different analytical tools. In terms of the current attitudes this would require an update to the Ethics Protocol.

In general the need to comply with the Ethics Protocol can sometimes delay the way the researcher discovers new sources of data and new ways of handling it. Some of these issues are discussed in Chapter 5.

This is not an attempt to provide a definitive list of potential paradoxes and contradictions which exist in the way that RECs function within universities, but rather it provides a few of the more obvious examples.

1.13 The Research Protocol - an essential prerequisite or a barrier to academic research?

As mentioned above academic research needs to be conducted to the highest ethical standards. It is in everyone's interest that this be the case. Without ethics awareness unsatisfactory practices can creep in and this can result in the research being tainted and thus regarded of little or no value.

However the way RECs currently function they are sometimes regarded by Faculty and research degree candidates as being a barrier to commencing the research as opposed to adding value to the research process. There is little doubt that ethical approval takes time and that the extra time required alone constrains the research. There is also much anecdotal evidence that some RECs make arbitrary decisions and request information and require processes that are not appropriate. However when an Ethics Protocol has been approved by a REC the researcher can have a higher degree of confidence that the proposed research will not run into trouble from an ethics point of view. This is a great advantage to the researcher in that he or she can be confident that if the procedures are followed there should be not be any ethics problems later in the research.

It is critical to realise that ethics approval should not be regarded as a one time event which can be attended to and then quietly forgotten. Annual ethics reviews help to prevent this. Providing courses which focus on delivering transferable skills in the subject of research ethics are needed for both potential researchers and for those who are involved in the processes required to conduct competent and efficient ethics reviews.

Different universities have different requirements for the certification of the compliance with the Ethics Protocol. In the case of research for a degree a certificate usually needs to be submitted with the dissertation. The most frequent requirement is a simple written statement made by the degree candidate that all the provisions of the Ethics Protocol have been complied with. However it needs to be understood that such a certification can only be given on the basis of stating that the Ethics Protocol has been complied with up to the point of the dissertation submission. It is normal to hold the data used in the research at least up to the point when it is examined and the degree is awarded. In fact in the past it was customary for academics to hold their data somewhat longer than that in case there was a challenge to the interpretation of it.

Chapter 2

What is research?

Ethics is in origin the art of recommending to others the sacrifices required for cooperation with oneself.

Bertrand Russell, (1976) A free man's worship and other essays', cited in *Columbia Dictionary of Quotations*, 1995, Columbia University Press, New York.

2.1 Introduction

There is an eerie feeling when defining research in a book such as this. One wonders whether everyone who will take this book in their hands thinks they know exactly what research is? However a debate about the boundaries of what could be called research, especially in as far as it concerns the REC, found that there was less agreement about this issue than there first appeared to be. Thus it is appropriate to pause and consider the question, *What is research?*

2.2 Teaching and Research activities

Universities generally make a distinction between teaching and research activities. Teaching activities are characterised by one way communication and are carried out in classrooms[18] in large groups and are supported by tutorials which are normally held with smaller groups. Where tutorial groups are small there is the opportunity to have two-way communications. Teaching aims to cover a previously determined curriculum over a fixed number of contact hours. Thus this is, by its nature, a structured event. As part of the teaching process students may be required to produce essays or papers on topics being addressed in the cur-

---

[18] Today a substantial amount of what used to be done in classrooms is delivered over the Internet through distance learning. Although the Internet and the Web have become vehicles for teaching delivery the principles of what is required of the student in order to learn is much the same as it has always been.

riculum. These will often require the examination of previously published papers and books. It may also require discussing with the lecturer and perhaps among students in a tutorial setting or even informally. This type of learning is generally not regarded as research.

In some instances, especially with part time students, an essay or assignment such as described above could be supported by information acquired from the student's employer. If this is a minor part of the work involved it would not be considered a research project.

Research activities can involve the student working on his or her own although there is also scope for research being conducted in groups. Research normally attempts to answer a question or series of questions, although it is possible that a research project could have as its objective the establishment of which questions should be asked. A more formal definition of academic research should include that it is a systematic investigation to establish a fuller understanding of a subject which may lead to being able to proclaim that something of value has been added to the body of knowledge.

Research does not have the structure of teaching as the researcher often sets his or her own agenda. However to be recognised as academic research the work should result in adding something new to the body of knowledge[19]. There is also a requirement in academic research for the work to have been conducted in a scholarly manner. Research is increasingly seen as an important tool for learning as it inevitably requires a high degree of focus and the researcher needs to find his or her own route to the answer.

2.3   Research – a variety of approaches

There is a wide variety of work which may be referred to as research and this ranges from library based activities, during which references to previously published material are sought for the exploration of the research

---

[19] When an undergraduate or for that matter an MBA student does a research project, the aim is to learn something about the subject and about how to write a research report. Their intention is not to add something of value to the body of knowledge, although sometimes this does actually happen. It is a serendipitous outcome.

issues, through to the setting up and use of experiments. Between these two extremes there are many alternatives available to the researcher in business and management studies and the number of ways of conducting research seems to be growing. There is potential for any approach to research to attract the attention of a REC, although not all forms of research will attract the same degree of ethics concern.

In the broadest sense of the word research involves the answering of a question or exploring an area for increased or new understanding. In the academic world research is characterised by being a process which is often seen as having three major stages. The first stage is the establishing of a suitable research question. The second stage is developing and implementing a research design and the third stage involves the analysis and the interpreting of the findings. The Ethics Protocol normally addresses issues relating to the research design. The extract below, from the Henley Business School, School of Management REC Briefing Notes, illustrates this point:-

> *...research involving human data or records. Ethical concerns are strongest where these data are gathered directly from the subject and then ethical approval is usually required. Where records are in the public domain, or where the subject is deceased, ethical considerations may still be relevant but such research does not normally require ethical approval;*

It is interesting to note how the words *usually* and *normally* are used which give the University scope to pursue different policies depending on the precise circumstances it faces. This definition could be criticised for being a catch all which could be replaced by the statement, *"All research requires ethics approval"*. By taking a broad view of research a university positions itself to be able to address the most innovative of research designs.

Not all scholarly activity should be considered research and therefore it follows that not all scholarly work will require an Ethics Protocol. However as RECs within most, if not every Faculty or School within a university, are becoming commonplace, it is wise to be aware of the issues which such Committees address[20].

2.4 Distinctions used by the NHS

The issue of what constitutes research is clearly important as it is a fulcrum around which the Ethics Protocol and REC functions. One interesting approach to the definition of research has been presented by the National Health Service (NHS) in the UK which has created a table showing a series of question answering activities and categorising the answers as either research or audit or evaluation. This can be seen in Figure 2.1.

For research to attract the attention of the REC it needs to have been conducted for the purposes of a degree such as a masters or doctorate or with the intention of being published in a Journal or on the Web. Research conducted entirely privately which will not be examined or published is only a matter of private concern[21].

Research	Clinical Audit	Service Evaluation
The attempt to define generalisable new knowledge including studies that aim to generate hypotheses as well as studies that aim to test them.	Designed and conducted to produce information to inform delivery of best care.	Designed and conducted solely to define or judge current care
Quantitative research - designed to test a hypothesis. Qualitative research – identifies/explores themes following established methodology.	Designed to answer the question: *"Does this service reach a predetermined standard?"*	Designed to answer the question: *"What standard does this service achieve?"*

Figure 2.1: Differentiating audit, service evaluation and research in the UK NHS.

Figure 2.1 is useful as it points out that there are several types of enquiry which are not considered, at least by the NHS in the UK, to be research. Universities could do well to pick up on these definitions for if they do not then there will be a tendency for university RECs to regard

---

[20] Private research would still have to comply with legislation such as the Data Protection Act.

[21] This statement assumes that the private research would not have contravened any of the laws relating to such issues as the DPA etc.

audits and evaluations as being research. This would encumber the university Committee unnecessarily.

With regards to the issue of writing books and to support academic teaching, these should not need an Ethics Protocol. However books which are based on research activities would normally have had an Ethics Protocol approval.

It is difficult to define research and it is more difficult to provide specific rules about which research projects require approval from the REC. As a result researchers should regard all research projects as requiring an Ethics Protocol and thus be prepared to have their proposed work examined by the REC.

Chapter 3

How Research Ethics evolved

In recent years ethical considerations across the research community have come to the forefront. This is partly a consequence of legislative change in human rights and data protection, but also a result of increased public concern about the limits of inquiry.

Ethical Guidelines, Social Research Association, 2003

3.1   RECs originate from medical research

The approaches to Ethics Protocols used in universities today have been developed from the thinking behind medical research and it is therefore useful to understand how and why medical ethics have developed as they did. In fact without understanding the context in which these RECs developed the whole procedure can look bizarre. This chapter is a high level overview of how attitudes have developed and changed over the years and where we stand today with regards to this challenging subject.

3.2   The starting point

Although there was some concern for research ethics in antiquity, as we understand it today, research ethics is really a 20th century concern. It is correct that the ancient Greeks were aware of the potential of medicine for good and for evil and thus the Hippocratic Oath was developed. Some centuries later there was concern about the use of cadavers in medical research which led the most eminent medical researcher of his time to declare that the anatomy of humans and pigs were the same. This was Claudius Galen and his writings on human anatomy based on what he knew about pigs were required reading for doctors for a thousand years until Andreas Vesalius in 1543 broke ranks and wrote his book "The Structure of the Human Body".

It was the Second World War that brought medical ethics to the attention of the world. The Second World War deeply affected social norms of what was and what was not acceptable in medical research. The war required many soldiers to travel to distant parts of the world and subject themselves to diseases they would not otherwise have come into contact with. Malaria, dysentery, yellow fever and in some cases gonorrhoea were major problems for the armed forces. Experiments were conducted with the blessing of the Roosevelt government which appointed medical research boards. The media and the public congratulated the medical world and participants for their contribution to the war effort. During this period the research subjects were not only volunteers but included prisoners and mentally ill patients in government facilities. Some reports suggest that the 1940s and 1950's were a period of an ethical vacuum but this was not always the case (for examples see Box 1).

Box 1 – War Time Experimentation

Dr Alf Alving from the University of Chicago conducted a 60 bed clinical trial on psychotic patients, injecting them with malaria. **No consent was requested.** He also used 500 inmates from the Stateville Penitentiary (an entire floor and part of one other). The fact that the prison 'volunteers' all came from the same floors indicates that they were not really volunteers at all - the Warden was known to co-operate with researchers.

Research on gonorrhoea funded and approved through the Committee on Medical Research (CMR) was conducted on a group of prisoners in Indiana. Prior to the research **there was some discussion on ethics and procedures** to be adopted to satisfy principles of voluntary participation and informed consent. However, the research never got off the ground because penicillin was established as a cure for the illness, providing no continuing need for the research to be conducted. Therefore the ethical guidelines were never established. See Box 3 'The Tuskegee Scandal' regarding a similar experiment that was handled in a different manner.

Research into dysentery was a key programme due to the effects of dysentery on the soldiers. There were several research grants given by the Committee on Medical Research (CMR) into this area. In many of these cases the experimentation was on institutionalised retarded people. There is **no evidence** that the CMR was concerned **about gaining informed consent** from people with a learning difficulty.

At some philosophical level, war, both the Second World War and the Cold War of the 1950s, may have promoted in the minds of the government and society as a whole, the idea of the greatest good for the greatest number of people, including justifying sending conscripts to war and experimenting on those in prison and institutions.

3.3   Post World War II

Between 1945 and 1946 the Nuremberg tribunal heard cases against 23 doctors and scientists on charges of murder in concentration camps. The victims of these murders were used as research subjects. Fifteen of these doctors were convicted. Another charge brought against these doctors was experimentation on human subjects without obtaining the subjects 'informed consent'. Even though these trials were run under the auspices of the United States (officially the trials are called *United States of America v. Karl Brandt et al.*), within the USA there was little concern that the lessons from these trials had any application to non-Nazi doctors.

The USA medical establishment focused on the fact that it was German Nazis supported by their Nazi government who committed these crimes. Therefore, the medical establishment saw this as a reason to consider government regulation of medicine and experimentation as not relevant to themselves. Indeed, in the USA there was little press coverage of the trials, so the research establishment and the public were not fully aware of the ethical issues being raised at Nuremberg.

The trials culminated in the Nuremberg Code[22] in 1948 as shown in Box 2. It is interesting to note that the Japanese doctors who conducted research on mostly Chinese victims were not tried for war crimes[23] by the USA as the 'Nazi doctors' were. Some of these criminals were tried by the Soviet forces at the Khabarovsk War Crime Trials[24] and received prison sentences.

Partly as a consequence of the lack of awareness by the public and partly because the medical profession in the USA did not view the Nuremberg

---

[22] http://ohsr.od.nih.gov/guidelines/nuremberg.html

[23] http://members.iinet.net.au/~gduncan/massacres_pacific.html

[24] Boris G. Yudin, Research on humans at the Khabarovsk War Crimes Trial, in: *Japan's Wartime Medical Atrocities: Comparative Inquiries in Science, History, and Ethics (Asia's Transformations)*, Jing Bao Nie, Nanyan Guo, Mark Selden, Arthur Kleinman (Editors); Routledge, 2010.

Code as being relevant to all doctors, medical research in the USA continued as before.

Box 2 - The Nuremberg Code

1. The voluntary consent of the human subject is absolutely essential.
2. The experiment should be such as to yield fruitful results for the good of society, unprocurable by other methods or means of study, and not random and unnecessary in nature.
3. The experiment should be so designed and based on the results of animal experimentation and a knowledge of the natural history of the disease or other problem under study that the anticipated results will justify the performance of the experiment.
4. The experiment should be so conducted as to avoid all unnecessary physical and mental suffering and injury.
5. No experiment should be conducted where there is a prior reason to believe that death or disabling injury will occur; except, perhaps, in those experiments where the experimental physicians also serve as subjects.
6. The degree of risk to be taken should never exceed that determined by the humanitarian importance of the problem to be solved by the experiment.
7. Proper preparations should be made and adequate facilities provided to protect the experimental subject against even remote possibilities of injury, disability, or death.
8. The experiment should be conducted only by scientifically qualified persons. The highest degree of skill and care should be required through all stages of the experiment of those who conduct or engage in the experiment.
9. During the course of the experiment the human subject should be at liberty to bring the experiment to an end if he *(sic)* has reached the physical or mental state where continuation of the experiment seems to him *(sic)* to be impossible.
10. During the course of the experiment the scientist in charge must be prepared to terminate the experiment at any stage, if he *(sic)* has probable cause to believe, in the exercise of the good faith, superior skill and careful judgement required of him *(sic)* that a continuation of the experiment is likely to result in injury, disability, or death to the experimental subject.

The public were still uncritical of medical research because of the many successes during and immediately after WWII. The National Institute of Health[25] (NIH), which took over much of the role of the CMR, which was disbanded after the war, was comprised of medical researchers (not practicing doctors) in leadership positions. Therefore experimentation, not the care of the patient, was viewed as the most important challenge. This led to a mindset of 'the ends justifying the means' with the researchers themselves judging what was right and wrong. In their view, history shows us that the improved outcomes scored strongly on the scale of what was considered 'right'.

Through the 1950s there was little philosophical discussion about medical ethics other than debates between doctors concerned with medical etiquette (i.e. how doctors should behave towards each other and their rights and responsibilities – not how to behave towards patients). Indeed for some historians, the American Medical Association's code of ethics was actually more like a set of trade union rules with little reference to the issue of ethics. Medical students learnt the subject of ethics by observation of their mentors, not as a subject of study in medical school. One author who took a different view (although his book was not noticed at the time) was Joseph Fletcher[26]. Fletcher took what was considered at the time as a "protestant view" towards the subject of ethics and tried to analyse the patient's point of view. He felt that doctors should tell patients the truth about their diagnoses so that the patient could be part of the process of making a choice about their own treatment.

3.4   The 1960's and 70's - Involving the subjects

In the 1960s Dr Louis Welt[27] conducted surveys of NIH research showing that few research departments had any procedural documents in place to review the ethics of human experimentation. In further research he showed that in the few instances where RECs existed they only had an advisory role - the decisions were ultimately with the researcher.

---

[25] http://www.nih.gov/
[26] http://home.earthlink.net/~rlindbeck/fletcher.htm#Biography
[27] http://www.ncbi.nlm.nih.gov/pmc/articles/PMC2595172/pdf/yjbm00150-0009.pdf

3.6 The Belmont Report

In 1979 a particularly influential report was issued which is referred to as the Belmont Report which further supported the ideas promulgated in the Nuremberg and Helsinki reports. In addition this report suggested that research should have beneficence for participants. This idea proposes that the research project should deliver some direct benefit to the research participants. This is to be encouraged but it is clear that not all research can bring benefits to the participants. For example, a researcher may explore criminal behaviour and the outcome of the research may or may not have the effect of preventing the participant from engaging in this type of activity.

3.7 Beecher and Pappworth

There were two key medical professionals who questioned the status quo of the medical profession at that time and these were Henry Beecher in the USA and Maurice Pappworth[32] in the UK. In 1962 Pappworth published 14 examples of medical research in the UK which did not comply with the Nuremberg Code. Later in 1967 he exposed 205 experiments and cited people and institutions in his book *Human Guinea Pigs*. Of these, 78 were in NHS hospitals. Henry Beecher in the USA submitted a paper citing 50 cases of bad practice to the Journal of the American Medical Association but they would not publish it. Later in 1966 he revised the article and reduced the number of cases to 22, of which two were from the UK, submitting it to the New England Journal of Medicine[33], who did publish the paper. Beecher informed the press about its publication to gain greater awareness of the issues amongst the public.

---

[32] Maurice Pappworth qualified to be a member of the Royal College of Physicians in 1936 but was prevented from joining because of his nationality / religion. This had implications for his career and mostly he worked as a tutor to other consultants. His lack of membership denied him hospital consultancy positions and this was said by the college to be because *"no Jew could ever be a gentleman"*. He was only awarded membership 57 years after his qualification. Note from the authors - *We have decided to include this remarkable comment about Pappworth as a Jew to illustrate the amazing prejudice of his times. Prejudice was rampant in our society against minorities, women, people who* did not speak with a received accent, to mention only a few groups.
[33] http://www.nejm.org/

In his paper Beecher separated the role of a doctor (whose concern was for individual patients) from that of a researcher whose aim was to advance knowledge and therefore was less concerned with individual patients. He also recognised the pressure on researchers to publish and that this may lead to disregarding a subject's rights. He did not offer suggestions for protocols as he still believed in the integrity of the researcher.

The culmination of the Beecher publication, the Southam lawsuit and the Livingstone Investigation in the USA, moved the NIH to alter their policies. They started to recognise that clinical research departs from the 'normal' doctor / patient relationship and therefore the experiment may not always be in the patient's best interest. They issued guidelines in July 1966 applicable to federally funded research involving human subjects. These guidelines assigned responsibility to the institute receiving the grant to keep evidence of informed consent, and to review the investigator's judgement by the use of an Institutional Review Board[34] (IRB) looking at the rights/welfare of the individual, risks, benefits of the trial and the method of gaining informed consent. These guidelines assigning responsibility to institutions for ethical matters have a deep resonance with what we now see as ethical review boards in the wider academic scene beyond medicine.

However, the definition of informed consent was still not what we think of today. The NIH brochures seeking volunteers for research stated "*You will be asked to sign a statement in which you indicate that you understand the project and agree to participate in it. If you find your assigned project to be intolerable, you may withdraw from it*". No other reason was offered to volunteers as acceptable for withdrawal from research!

In August 1966 the Federal Drugs Administration (FDA) in the USA went further than the NIH and issued their statement on policy concerning consent for the use of investigational new drugs on humans which distinguished between therapeutic and non-therapeutic research (as did the Helsinki Declaration) and importantly they clarified the meaning of consent. The FDA defined consent as when a person received a "*fair explanation*" of the procedure and was thus able to exercise choice. The

---

[34] The name given to an Ethics Review Committee based in a teaching facility where research is conducted.

of the 1970's a survey showed that about 90% of medical practitioners reported that they would tell a patient if there was a diagnosis of cancer whereas a previous survey at the end of the 1960's showed that 90% of the profession would not disclose this fact to the patient. A key point of principle to emerge through the 1970's was that ethical decisions could not be left to the profession and that these decisions should be made by RECs drawn from a wide sphere including the public. One of the concomitant effects, argued through the American court system, was that this would spread the liability of 'bad decisions' away from the doctor, if he / she followed the advice of an Ethic Committee. However at this stage, many hospitals still did not set up IRBs as there was no compunction to do so within the *National Research Act 1974*. At the core of the public outcry, which in effect supported the introduction of RECs and the Law Courts' decisions, was the establishment of the rights of the individual (or where incapable, their family) to make their own decision in all circumstances. Of course an individual cannot make an informed decision without access to all the relevant knowledge available.

3.9   New Diseases - New Concerns

The 1980's brought several major 'new' diseases. The AIDs crisis hit the world. From 1985 Bovine Spongiform Encephalopathy (BSC) was prevalent amongst cattle in the UK and by 1994 Variant Creutzfeldt-Jakob Disease (vCJD) had infected the first human. The lack of certainty that one was receiving a 'clean' blood product when given a transfusion, again bought ethical issues to the fore. The primary issue for ethicists concerned the privacy of a patients' information, e.g., if they are diagnosed with AIDs, HIV, vCJD or other diseases such as hepatitis and sexually transmitted diseases. Medical procedures were not put in place fast enough to prevent infection of both HIV and vCJD amongst patients. Unlike the 1960's and 1970's these issues were not kept hidden until someone like Beecher blew the whistle. As well as the broadening media, the use of computers and the introduction of the internet led to widespread public input into the debates in medical, legal, religious and political spheres. The time for ethics to be discussed within the confines of the profession alone had gone forever. Whilst the issue of informed consent had been entrenched in UK law since the 1960's it had not kept pace with public opinion or with technology and medical techniques. It is only in the last decade or so that universities generally (i.e. beyond medical schools) have been adopting the same principles.

3.10 Principles guiding research

These principles are do no harm, gain informed consent (including full disclosure), assure privacy of data and offer the absolute right to withdraw from any research activity. Interestingly, the emphasis is a priori. That is, the REC is interested in the wording of the consent forms, the processes proposed etc. The REC cannot monitor the progress of the research other than by performing periodic audits (normally annually).

How effective can this be? After all we still hear of violations of public trust from the medical profession. In 2001 it became public knowledge that the Alder Hay Hospital in Liverpool had been harvesting hearts from children who died prior to the bodies being returned to their parents. Doctors and other medical professionals had known about this 'store' of parts for some time[36].

Surplus skin from plastic surgery in breast and abdominal operations was sold by the Salisbury Health Care Trust to the Defence Evaluation Research Agency at Porter Down where it was used for chemical weapons research without the patients' knowledge or consent[37].

In Ireland, drug companies including Pharmacia Ireland (now part of Pfizer) and Novo Nordisk admitted to paying for dead infant glands without the parents consent[38]

It needs to be stated that it is not only medical science which has a record of questionable research practice. Punch (1996) points to 10 cases of corporate misconduct including the manipulation of research findings in the Goodrich brakes scandal and the Turkish Airlines DC-10 door problems leading to the crash in the Bois de Boulogne near Paris. The misconduct described by Punch (1996) ranged far wider than research practice and thus pointed out how easy it is to neglect the ethics issues in a business situation.

---

[36] (http://news.bbc.co.uk/1/hi/1136723.stm)
[37] (http://www.dailymail.co.uk/news/article-22015/Spare-skin-sold-weapons-tests.html)
[38] (http://www.bioedonline.org/news/news.cfm?art=1294).

The above examples of medical experimentation and practice, provides some logic to the processes that the medical profession followed. They have focused on Anglo-American bioethical events, but it should not be interpreted that this was only of concern to the Western countries. Bio-ethics is an international issue, crossing geographical and cultural boundaries, leading to different interpretations. Despite this possible limitation it helps us understand the nature of what we, as researchers, are being asked to do by RECs. It does not however, suggest whether these procedures are the correct ones for business and management research.

3.11   The knock-on effect

In the late 1990's universities, beyond medical schools, started to apply Ethics Protocols to the processes asked of university researchers. Initially this was for postgraduate research degrees but the requirement has now been extended to most graduate degrees (including taught masters) and in some cases also to research conducted by undergraduates. It has led to the situation now where it is the norm to require researchers of all types to write ethics applications. This has become a substantial administrative burden for some universities and this is why in some cases the supervisor has had to take on the function of a REC. This has added a new layer of responsibility to students, supervisors and examiners and implies that most academics will have been trained either by attending classes or by self-study to understand the ethics issues involved.

3.12   From medical schools to business schools

The Ethics Protocol required by most business schools has been strongly influenced by the medical ethics history described above. It requires researchers to show that they are not harming their informants, are getting informed consent and are not deceiving the participants, are giving full information, permitting withdrawal from the research at any time and ensuring the informants privacy. Researchers are responsible to the institution for their conduct. The institution will not give a blanket authority to research.

When the universities decided that research governance was an issue of concern to them, they based their policies on the assumption that *any* research that was "involving human participants" should be directly answerable to the guardians of ethics. However the term "involving human participants" can be broadly interpreted to include every research encounter with a human. This interpretation is possibly an over reaction bearing in mind the type of research normally conducted in business schools. In a sense all researchers within universities are paying for the 'sins' of the medical researchers. University faculty have been accustomed to being responsible to themselves for their own sense of intellectual integrity, and this has been the cornerstone of academic freedom. Whether the interpretation of "involving human participants" is the correct one for use in business research, is a debate for another occasion. The lessons from medical research are still relevant today in that they are still referred to and are what govern research ethics at present.

3.13 What society learned from the poor practice in medical research

There are a number of learning points which arise from the sorry tale of medical research practices from the period of the Second World War onwards. Some of these are as follows:

- No harm should ever come to a human being as a result of participating in a research project. Participants should be in no way worse off, physically, emotionally or intellectually after the research than before it.
- No human being should ever be coerced into being part of any research without his or her freely given consent. This means that the person involved should be fully informed of all the relevant facts concerning the objective of the research and also be given a thorough briefing about any possible dangers which might result from the research or as a consequence of the research. Participants should give their consent to participate in the research in writing. If the individuals are not literate (or for some other reason have difficulty in understanding the details of a Letter of Informed Consent) then special arrangements have to be made so that the researcher can be confident that they have agreed to participate in the research.
- Research participants have to be given the right to withdraw from the research without having to give any justification other then they have changed their minds. Whatever data they have supplied has to be removed from the research finding, if it is

possible to so do. It is possible that a research participant's data has been anonymised and entered into a database and in this case it may not be possible to indentify the data concerned.

- Any data collected about human beings should be used for only the stated purpose of the research and for no other purpose without obtaining the explicit permission of the informants.
- All the data collected should be held confidentially and securely and should be destroyed after the research has been completed.

It is these lessons which have underpinned medical research and which have now been applied to academic research outside of the medical faculties.

It should also be noted that some of these lessons, such as data should only be used for the original purpose and data should be deleted when the purpose has been fulfilled, have found themselves incorporated in Data Protection legislation as described in Chapter 6

Chapter 4

Ethics Protocol application

Integrity without knowledge is weak and useless, and knowledge without integrity is dangerous and dreadful.

Samuel Johnson, The astronomer, in *The History of Rasselas,* ch. 41 (1759).

4.1   Management of research

It is important for an academic researcher to understand how research is managed in their Faculty, School or Department. Managing research is a relatively new concept in universities which were famous for their lack of management and control of the activities of their staff. This lack of control was well described by the playful question, *How do you define a university?* Which was answered by the statement that *A university is an institution where all the staff share a common car park!* If nothing else this conveys the lack of control which universities had over the activities of its staff or Faculty. Also in some universities the car park answer was not true as car parking was only provided for Senior Lecturers and above and a car parking space was seen as a symbol of position in the hierarchy of the university.

In recent years universities have had to improve their management and control procedures. In some cases this has led to a considerable amount of resentment from the older members of staff who decry the university efforts as creeping managerialism. However these individuals are increasingly in the minority as management practices are introduced to universities at all levels including Faculty, School and Department.

With regards to research, each Faculty, School or Department will have a Director of Postgraduate Studies. The Office of the Director of Postgraduate Studies will normally ensure that the details of the Ethics Protocol requirements are included in the papers provided to all students when their registration is approved. These papers will provide guidance to prospective researchers and point out to them that Ethics Protocol approval should be sought by the time that their research proposal has been formally submitted. Some universities require that formal permission to use an Ethics Protocol has been granted before the research proposal can be finally accepted. It may be noted that there is the potential to have a chicken and egg situation here.

The Director of Postgraduate Studies has a number of functions, one of which will be to keep a record of research proposals which postgraduates are interested in pursuing. These proposals will have to be agreed upon by supervisors or in some cases the Director of Postgraduate Studies himself or herself. At this stage it is useful to ensure that the Ethics Protocol issues are formally raised and that ethics permission is requested. For masters degrees the process should normally be routine and the application should be reviewed and completed within a month or so. At doctoral level the period required may be a little longer. This does depend on the complexity of the research and in some cases the application for permission may have to be submitted a number of times before the REC is fully satisfied. Where multiple RECs become involved, as described in the case study in Chapter 6, the period required to complete an Ethics Protocol approval may extend over several months. It is possible that a research project will not obtain approval and will have to be abandoned. This fortunately does not happen often.

Faculties, Schools and Departments are increasingly asking to be informed as to what staff who are not registered for a degree are planning to research in the forthcoming year. This information is required for several reasons including that it allows the Dean, Head of School or Head of Department to see what type of issues will be studied. This is the first step in tracking research activity within the university and thus it may be seen as opening a conversation regarding Ethics Protocols.

4.2   The objective of the Ethics Protocol

It is useful to bear in mind that this whole exercise of preparing an application for approval is driven by the requirement that researchers should:-

- do no harm to either participants or to the researchers themselves;
- acquire informed consent after full disclosure[39];
- collect the data in an acceptable way;
- protect the privacy of data and retain it only as long as is necessary;
- make clear the absolute right to withdraw from any research and have their data removed from the records.

4.3   Getting the application going

There will be occasions when the research is based on archival records and no ethics approval will be required. In such cases the Dean, Head of School or Head of Department will normally be able to allow the research to proceed. However in most cases there will be some ethics approval required and this means that an application needs to be made to the REC. Application forms differ considerably and it is important that the researcher obtains a copy and studies it carefully. An application form has been supplied in Exhibit A to show the detail required. The application for ethics approval normally consists of a self completion form which needs to be submitted together with a number of supporting documents which are discussed below.

Application forms will usually address the following:-

- A declaration or certification section;
- Personal details of the researcher and any others who may be involved with the research;
- The title of the research project[40];
- The purpose of the research;

---

[39] Full disclosure and informed consent is the ideal to which all researchers should aspire. But there are occasions when this is not a simple issue. For example, how does one resolve informed consent requirements with the research of institutional racism or sexism. The moment it is known that this is the agenda then it is most unlikely that the researcher will be welcomed by the research participant or subject, or his or her organisation.
[40] Some universities require the research proposal to be submitted together with the application for ethics approval. Other universities require evidence of the ethics approval before the proposal is finally accepted.

- How the data will be acquired;
- A list of any other formal permission which may be required;
- Details of informants who will be approached and how they will be approached and how the data will be collected;
- Details of confidentiality assurances which will be given;
- Details of how the data will be stored during the research and how it will be disposed of thereafter.

Some application forms are no more than a page or two but others are highly structured and will thus be spread over 6, 8, 10 or more pages.

4.3.1 The declaration or certification section

This section of the application form requires the researcher, and in the case of multiple researchers, the lead researcher to certify that:-

- he, she or they are responsible for the manner in which they conduct the research;
- he, she or they have familiarised themselves with the university's research ethics guidelines;
- he, she or they are familiar with the ethics of their own field of study;
- he, she or they, where applicable, have consulted the Data Protection Legislation; and
- all the data and documentation supplied are true and correct.

It is important to bear in mind that the responsibility for the proper conduct of the research rests with the researcher and where there is more than one researcher, then the lead researcher.

When the researcher signs this document he or she is certifying that certain actions have already taken place, such as that the researcher has already familiarised him or herself with the Data Protection Legislation and the researcher is formally committing himself or herself to the other actions which are specified in the documents. Such a form should not be signed lightly.

4.3.2 Personal details of the researcher and any others who may be involved with the research.

This section may include details of contact numbers, e-mail, street address, university student or staff number etc.

4.3.3 The title of the research project

At this stage the title supplied may be a working title which might change subsequently. If a major change is made to the title, especially if this represents a change in methodology, then the researcher may have to reapply for a revised Ethics Protocol. As this would require a considerable amount of time and effort, changes should be avoided if possible.

4.3.4 The purpose of the research

This will normally be either for the purposes of obtaining a degree or for publication in a peer reviewed journal. The research specified in the application could be part of a bigger research programme and if this is the case it should be stated here.

As a research proposal is often part of the approval application members of the Committee may require further access to information on the purpose of the research. There should be no second agendas. If the openness of the researcher comes into question the informants will not trust the researcher and this will result in the creditably of the data being questioned.

When a member of faculty wishes to undertake a private research project there may be no need to obtain REC approval. However if the individual wants to suggest that there is an association between the research being conducted and the university then ethics approval should be sought.

It is possible that there could be a covert research agenda where the researcher wishes to explore an issue which will not be freely discussed by the informants. This does not happen much in the field of business and management studies. However, an example of this could be if a researcher wanted to explore a research question related to hard, "foot-in-the-door" type selling or some form of advertising which was potentially not entirely honest. A REC could give its approval to this type of research provided no harm came to the informants. It is customary for the researcher to explain in a debriefing meeting the nature of the deception to any informant who had been so deceived. This requirement might be withdrawn from the protocol if it was obvious that the informant would immediately ask to have his or her data removed. It is always extremely difficult to obtain approval for an Ethics Protocol which involves deceit of any sort.

4.3.5   How the data will be acquired

Here the researcher needs to specify if interviews, questionnaires, focus groups or participant-observer techniques will be employed – to mention only a few possibilities.

This is a particularly important part of the Ethics Protocol and as much detail as possible should be given at this point. The researcher should not only explain how the data will be gathered but also give a rationale as to why the approach suggested is the most effective way of obtaining the data.

If a questionnaire is to be used then a copy of the questionnaire needs to be provided. If interviews are involved then the researcher needs to supply interview schedules for each type of interview.

In the case of a focus group then the Committee will expect to see the focus group protocol.

4.3.6   A list of any other formal permission which may be required

As well as obtaining Letters of Informed Consent from each individual informant, it is sometimes necessary for the researcher to obtain permission from a higher level in the organisation. For example, if the researcher is interviewing a group of sales people in an organisation, he or she should have a letter of permission from a senior executive agreeing that the sales people can give the researcher the time to supply the information required.

As mentioned before, if children are involved a police clearance is also required. If the researcher is to work with dangerous substances then clearance from the Health and Safety authorities and perhaps other regulatory bodies may be needed. If the researcher is intending to travel abroad then another level of permission is required from the university.

4.3.7 Details of informants who will be approached and how they will be approached

This section requires that the researcher has thought through the type of people required to supply the data. For example, the research might require data from senior human resources managers. Having established this, the researcher then needs to consider how these people may be approached. If cold calls are made, it is likely that the researcher will obtain a low rate of success in soliciting data. On the other hand if the researcher can identify a gatekeeper who will support the researcher's project then the likelihood of success has been substantially increased. The subject of gatekeepers is more fully explored in Chapter 7).

Some research approval applications require details of the informants such as the number of people, their age, their gender, exclusion and inclusion criteria. Then the researcher needs to point out why certain potential informants would be suitable and why others might not. In addition some research approval applications require a statistical justification for the number of informants sought.

On the question of how informants will be approached to participate in the study, this will depend on the research question and methodological options which are taken. In general RECs are not enthusiastic about rewards being offered to informants for contribution to the research.

If contractors are to be used in assisting in the data collection then it has to be made clear that the assistants will be given appropriate training and that adequate supervision will be put in place.

The same principles apply if the researcher wishes to use helpers with data capture and data vetting for the purposes of computer processing.

4.3.8 Details of confidentiality assurances which will be given

It is a fundamental axiom that researchers need to reassure informants that whatever they say during an interview, a focus group or on any other occasion related to the research, their opinions will be regarded as given in confidence[41].

Most researchers have little trouble in complying with this requirement. However there are occasions when the researcher is obliged by law to inform the authorities regarding information received. The law requires information to be supplied to the police if the researcher becomes aware of any activity concerning money laundering or activities related to terrorism[42].

It is important that the researcher understand that the law does not recognise a privileged relationship between the researcher and the informant and that if called upon to supply information the researcher will have to comply with such a demand or face criminal charges[43].

In the normal course of events the researcher will simply give assurances in writing both in the Participants Information Document and in the Letter of Consent to the affect that any information supplied will not be passed on to others and that the information acquired will be used in such a way that the informant will not be identified.

4.3.9 *How the data will be stored during the research and how it will be disposed of thereafter*

Assurances of confidentiality may be of limited value if the data obtained is not stored securely and out of sight of people who are not directly involved in the research. Therefore it is important to state that the data will be securely stored on a computer with ID and password control, etc.

---

[41] This can be problematic with focus groups as the assurance of confidentiality is given by other members of the focus group. Chatham House Rules is the term used to describe a situation where all the members of the group agree not to attribute any comments made to any particular person.

[42] It is not obligatory for the researcher to report any other type of misconduct to the authorities.

[43] Only information disclosed between husband and wife and between patient and doctor and priest and confessant are considered privileged. Journalists would like to be considered in this category with regards to their informants but they are not.

It is good practice to anonymise the data as soon as possible and if references to the individuals are not required then there is no point in retaining records which show individual informant's names.

The filing cabinet and the room in which the records are stored should be as a matter of course locked when not in use.

4.4   Supporting documents

The application form will be submitted together with other supporting documents and these may include inter alia:-

- The research proposal;
- The proposed measuring or data collection instruments;
- The participant's information document;
- The Letter of Informed consent;
- Copies of other relevant permissions;
- Copies of other consent forms such as consent to have an interview recorded;
- Police clearance where necessary;
- Guardian consent form/s if relevant.

Some universities will require multiple copies of the application form and the accompanying documents which may have to be submitted on paper as well as electronically.

4.4.1 The research proposal

Not all universities will require the research proposal to be submitted to the REC as it is a substantial task to read such a document. As this document should already have been submitted to other officers of the university, it would be available if it is subsequently required.

The research proposal will spell out in some detail the research methodology and its rationale.

A summary of the research proposal is often adequate for the purposes of the REC provided the other issues described here are adequately addressed.

4.4.2 The proposed measuring instruments

A measuring instrument is at the centre of any research project and thus is a critical document in the ethics risk assessment. Any criticism of a measuring instrument directly impinges on the research methodology and some researchers have suggested that this effectively allows the REC to be critical of more than only the ethics issues.

If a questionnaire is being used then the Ethics Protocol will need to justify why, how the instrument has been designed, and how the different parts of the questionnaire function to facilitate the answering of the research questions. This can be quite challenging as members of the REC can have a variety of views on an issue such as this. It is important for the researcher to justify his or her claims.

The same thinking applies to interview schedules which will be used during semi-structured interviews.

The REC will scrutinise questionnaires and interview schedules to ensure that no improper questions are going to be asked of informants. It is difficult to define an improper question. Some informants may find a question asking for their racial group to be improper. Others may find a question relating to age to be unacceptable. It is wise to avoid a question related to salary and to religion. A question on political affiliation or on sexual preference would not be advised.

4.4.3 The participant's information document

This document spells out for a potential informant the rationale of the research and why the researcher believes that the informant involvement will be helpful. Sometimes the participant's information document in an abbreviated form is included within the Letter of Informed Consent. Sometimes it is a separate document which is attached to the Letter of Informed Consent. Either way it is important that the potential informant reads this document and agrees in writing that he or she has done so. This may be seen in Appendix 1.

4.4.4 The Letter of Informed Consent

The Letter of Informed Consent can be a short letter which needs to be signed by the participant before data may be obtained from him or her. An example of this document is supplied in Appendix 2.

4.4.5   Copies of other relevant permissions

Where these have been required and obtained they should be attached to the application. If permissions have be applied for but not yet received then a letter indicating such can be supplied, but the permission will need to be subsequently presented.

4.4.6   Copies of other consent forms such as consent to have an interview recorded

A short letter of consent is required here. An example of this document is supplied in Appendix 3.

4.4.7   Police clearance where necessary

A document from the police authority is required here. Obtaining this can be a lengthy process and adequate time needs to be set aside for this. Such a clearance may take months rather than weeks[44].

4.4.8   A guardian consent form if relevant

Where children are involved this will be required. It should not be underestimated how long and how difficult it can be to obtain consent from a group of guardians or parents.

4.5   Ex-ante and ex-post

The discussion in this chapter has focused on the detail of what is required when completing an application for the approval of an Ethics Protocol. All of this has to be thought about and recorded in the application before the research can begin. Therefore the application represents how the researcher thinks the research will proceed and it is thus an ex-ante statement of intent.

Many RECs state that they can audit the progress of the research at any time they wish. Certainly this is an important aspect of ensuring high ethical standards. However it is not a trivial matter for a REC to audit a research programme. There is considerable work involved in such a pro-

---

[44] In some jurisdictions, such as Canada, a police clearance certificate can be obtained the same day.

ject and also it is not clear that there will be anyone on the REC who will have the competence to so do.

Other universities insist that the researcher sign an ex-post statement that he or she has complied with all the requirements as specified in the Ethics Protocol. The signing of such a document is a serious matter and if it were to be subsequently discovered that this statement was untrue then the degree which had been awarded on the basis of the statement could be in jeopardy.

4.6   Summary

It is not a trivial exercise to prepare an application for the approval of an Ethics Protocol. It is equally obvious that it is impossible to provide a set of universally applicable generic rules for this purpose. What is required to obtain approval is specific to each university and even to particular Faculties, Schools and Departments. The information required is also a function of the particular research project and how the researcher wishes to pursue his or her work.

A simple research ethics approval could take a number of days. A more complex one could require a number of weeks. There are always delays in waiting for the REC to convene. There may be considerably longer delays when external permissions are needed.

What is important is that time is set aside for this process and for becoming well informed about these issues.

One of the issues mentioned above was Data Protection Legislation. To become familiar with this alone is a substantial task and should not be left to the last minute.

Chapter 5

Amending the Ethics Protocol

*We do not act rightly because we have virtue or excellence, but
we rather have these attributes because we have acted rightly.*

Aristotle.

5.1   Introduction

Not only does a researcher need ethics permission at the outset of the
project but there is sometimes a need for an ongoing conversation between the researcher and the REC over the life of the project. This is due
to the fact that the circumstances of a research project can change, and
change several times over its duration. Unfortunately the way that the
application for approval for an Ethics Protocol is currently set up can
lead the researcher to feel that the ethics issue is a one off problem
which can be fixed by filling out a set of forms and supplying a number
of documents to the Committee. This is unfortunate as ethics permeates
the whole research project and really should be at the forefront of the
researcher's mind throughout the project. This is a new orientation for
business and management researchers and the realisation of the importance of ethics is still growing in this research community.

5.2   The need to get going

Once the initial Ethics Protocol has been approved the academic research may commence. If for any reason the project does not commence within 12 months, it is usual that the researcher has to reapply
for approval. This type of situation normally only occurs when there is
some problem with the funding of the research or the principle researcher has been taken ill or left the university.

5.3   Annual review

Research projects should be reviewed annually and the extent to which this happens will depend on the particular project and the circumstances of the university, the Faculty or the School. One of the key issues here is the volume of research being undertaken by the university. Some universities have a thousand or more masters students and hundreds of doctoral students[45] and where Ethics Protocols are required for undergraduates the problem becomes much greater. In such environments the burden of approving[46] and auditing all the active research protocols is such that only a small percentage of the Ethics Protocols may be audited each year. The annual review of the ethics application will address matters including:

- the continuity of the project;
- any unforeseen ethical issues which may have arisen in the course of the year relating to the project;
- what changes, if any, to the project methodology or its operation have taken place.

In most cases the above three issues will at most constitute minor changes if any and can be dealt with outside a formal meeting of a REC. Chairperson's action is usually adequate in these cases.

5.4   Amendments to the original ethics application

In addition to annual audits there is the question of amendments to the original ethics application arising from changes in the research itself. Academic research can experience changes to the research design as the work progresses. The question which then comes into play is *How these changes should be accommodated by or into the Ethics Protocol?* There are two types of amendments which may be made to an Ethics Protocol. These are substantial changes or amendments and minor or non-substantial changes or amendments. Substantial changes may require the researcher to reapply for approval of the Ethics Protocol while minor

---

[45] Larger universities will have several thousand master students and a thousand or more doctoral students.

[46] It is in these situations that supervisors are asked to take on the role of the Research Ethics Committee.

or non-substantial amendments do not. The challenge is, of course, being able to distinguish between the two.

5.5   Substantial changes or amendments

The following are some of the changes or amendments which would normally be considered as substantial.

- A change to the field of study or to the topic to be researched;
- A change in methodology;
- A change to the type of participants required for the research;
- Changes regarding a new site if the new location is abroad;
- Major changes to the documentation to be used during the research including a revision of a questionnaire or an interview schedule;
- Where team research is being undertaken a change in the principle researcher;
- An change which would affect the university's insurance position;
- A change to the expected outcome of the research.

The university will normally have a form which the researcher is required to submit to the REC which will contain all the information required to make a new decision. It is important to submit this information in the required format. As mentioned sometimes this will be signed off by the Chairperson without any further representations being required.

However, it is possible that a substantial change could require the research to be halted until it is considered by a full REC. There are examples of a proposed change causing the ethics approval to be withdrawn and the research project being abandoned.

5.6   Minor or non-substantial amendments

The following are some of the changes or amendments which would normally be considered as minor or non-substantial.

- Any changes required to remove minor errors such as typographical errors or spelling mistakes;

- Changes regarding the inclusion of a small number of additional questions in the questionnaires provided they do not change the meaning or the tone of the questionnaire;
- Extension of the period over which the research is to be conducted;
- Changes regarding a new site for the research provided it is not distinctly different from the other research sites;
- Changes regarding the inclusion of additional informants provided they are the same sort of people as previously agreed to.

It is clearly not easy to precisely define what would make an issue substantial as opposed to minor or vice versa.

5.7 The modus operandi

If the researcher is satisfied that the changes are minor then there is no requirement to resubmit an application for approval to the ethics Committee. If it is believed that the changes are major the researcher is required to inform the Chair of the REC who may be able to grant the researcher permission to proceed without having to present a new application.

Where the researcher is in any doubt he or she should always consult the Chairperson of the appropriate REC.

5.8 The challenge

The first challenge is that what may appear to one person as a minor amendment may appear to another individual as a substantial one. There is no easy way around this problem and the sensible way of handling this is to err on the side of caution. This will result in more change notification being made than is strictly necessary.

In addition the problem which many universities face is the challenge of being able to keep up with the dynamic processes of research when large numbers of researchers are involved. The way research is eventually conducted is seldom the same as was envisaged at the outset. Many research proposals are no more than a guess at what will happen during the research processes. The same applies to research protocols and this in turn directly affects Ethics Protocols. The way that researchers are required to submit applications for the approval of an Ethics Protocol suggests a greater degree of certainty about the way the research will be conducted than most researchers are able to honestly provide. Thus change to the Ethics Protocol is almost inevitable.

In examining the list of minor amendments above it is hard not to come to the conclusion that a masters student or even a novice doctoral research student could competently and confidently decide if any of these issues should be reported to the Chairperson of the REC. If only a supervisor is involved in agreeing the Ethics Protocol then the situation is even more tenuous. When this type of situation occurs there is a propensity for what is sometimes called the Jesuit Principle to emerge. The Jesuit Principle is sometimes summarised as, *It is easier to beg forgiveness than to ask permission*. This is not a satisfactory situation for the university and should be discouraged. But ethics approval and auditing is costly and a university can do no more than its resources allow.

Chapter 6

Data Protection Legislation

Relativity applies to physics, not ethics"

A Einstein

6.1   Introduction to data protection

Data protection legislation is important because a number of the provisions of this legislation have been incorporated directly into university requirements for the approval of Ethics Protocols.

By the early 1980s it was obvious that computers were beginning to play an increasingly influential role in civil society. Computer capacity had become bigger than anyone had ever dreamed. Their speed was thought to be breath taking. Their price-power ratio was declining and unusual boxes, called microcomputers, were beginning to appear on peoples' desks and in their homes. When IBM launched its PC in 1981 the wave of personal computer ownership could be seen as unstoppable.

The Thatcher Government in the United Kingdom decided that it had better support the inevitable development which would follow by announcing the United Kingdom Information Technology Year 1982 which was referred to as IT82. Large numbers of organisations gave their support to the promotion of the new technology as may be seen by the announcement of the English Spelling Society as follows:-

As this issue goes to press, the United Kingdom is well into its promotion and publicity for Information Technology Year 1982 when the British Government is spending £1.2 million to publicise modern developments in electronic communication, microprocessors, and video equipment.

All these were non-existent in their present forms only a few decades ago. Two hundred years ago, the only major piece of Infor-

57

mation Technology was the printed word. The basis for storing information was invented several thousand years ago - the writing system.

In 1982 there will be still more marvellous developments in modern communications. Not one modern marvel will remain unchanged, unimproved. What will be the modern developments in the writing system? How much and in what way will they be influenced by computers, electronic typewriters, and typesetters, etc.? All these are already here. They will be used to the fullest extent of their capabilities!

In the Proceedings of the Third International Conference on Spelling, Research and Reform, held in Edinburgh in July, 1981 and sponsored by the Simplified Spelling Society, the possibilities for development related to IT are made more clear and convincing.

In retrospect this looks rather naive but for its time it was forward thinking in that it envisaged that it would be necessary to cope with major developments in aspects of society related to data processing.

As well as the excitement about new hardware and software there was a growing realisation that there was a potential for really large increases in data and questions began to be asked concerning whether there was a need to control certain aspects of this data. The data which was of concern to those asking these questions was personal data about individuals.

It had been long established that the protection of privacy is a right of the individual and the collection of data, especially the large volume of data which was becoming possible with the development of Information Technology, was a concern. As a result the Data Protection Act (DPA) was introduced in the UK in 1984 and became law in 1985. The UK was not the first country to do this as Sweden had a Data Act from 1973. In 1998 a new Act was introduced in the UK as a result of an EU Data Protection Directive and the old 1984 Act was repealed.

Today many countries have enacted laws which regulate how data concerning people may be stored, processed, transferred and used. Although these laws differ from country to country there are common principles for the management of the data about which researchers should be aware. The application form for some Ethics Protocols require the researcher to certify that he or she is familiar with the provision of the relevant legislation and that the proposed work will comply with its provisions.

The DPA is a substantial piece of legislation and it has a reputation of being complex. Therefore from the point of view of an academic researcher it is best understood by reference to the principles which underpin it.

In addition there is in the UK a Freedom of Information Act which may have some impact on data held by researchers. However its impact is likely to be less than is the case with the DPA. The Freedom of Information Act supports openness and accountability, and allows individuals to call for documents, e-mails and notes held by individual staff members. If a request for information is refused then the applicant can initiate a complaints procedure.

6.2   DPA Principles

In the UK the DPA regulates the use of personal data and the Act is based on a number of principles which include the following:-

- Data may only be used for the purpose for which it was collected;
- Data may not be disclosed to other parties who are not involved with the original purpose for which the data was collected;
- Data should be held only for the time required to use it for its stated purpose;
- Adequate security measures should be in place for the storage of the data;
- Data may not be transferred outside the boundaries of the European Economic Area (EEA) unless the data is going to a country which has appropriate data protection legislation[47];
- Organisations which process data such as this need to be registered with the Information Commissioner's Office;

---

[47] The EEA includes the countries in the EU as well as Iceland, Liechtenstein and Norway.

- People whose data is being held have a right of access to the data;
- If there is factually incorrect data then the people about whom the data is being held have the right to have the data corrected.

The regulations of this Act only apply to data which refers to living and identifiable individuals.

Anonymised or aggregated data is not regulated under this Act. Therefore statistics alone do not fall within the purview of the Act.

For the Act to apply, data has to be held on a computer or in a relevant filing system. The notion of relevant filing systems allows/means that paper files may also fall under the purview of the Act.

As multinational research is on the increase the issue of data crossing boundaries is becoming more important. Besides EEA countries, the Data Protection Commissioners have nominated Argentina, Canada, Guernsey, Jersey, The Isle of Mann and Switzerland as countries which have adequate data protection laws in place to allow data transfer from the UK. Data transfer is allowed by the Data Commissioners to other countries provided that adequate contractual arrangements can be made.

There is one other issue which relates to the cross border requirements of the DPA and it is the use of products such as the Internet-based Survey Monkey. This online questionnaire development product retains and stores the data obtained from a questionnaire, without stating where the data is being processed and held. Whether Survey Monkey complies with the requirements of the Act would be unknown to the researcher.

6.3   Implications for the researcher

These principles impose restrictions on what the researcher may do with the data and how the researcher needs to deal with the informants who have supplied it in the first place. It is clear that these principles have influenced how universities think about research ethics.

6.3.1 Data may only be used for the purpose for which it was collected

Research degree candidates need to make clear at the outset why the data is required. Most individuals will immediately rush to declare that the data is only required for the purposes of a dissertation. This, of course, can be limiting if after the dissertation is complete the researcher wishes to pursue further research leading to publications in peer reviewed journals. If this is a possible requirement then it needs to be addressed in the Letter of Informed Consent.

6.3.2 Data may not be disclosed to other parties who are not involved with the original purpose for which the data was collected

Although the data collected could possibly be of use for other purposes besides the research objective specified in the Ethics Protocol, this is not allowed by the DPA or by the university. The scope of the work for which the data is collected may not be allowed to creep.

6.3.3 Data should be held only for the time required to use it for its stated purpose

Academics have been traditionally unclear about how long data should be held after the research is completed. Some academics have argued that data should be available for some time in case someone wanted to replicate the study. In terms of the DPA the data should be destroyed when the dissertation is accepted and the subsequent papers are published.

6.3.4 Adequate security measures should be in place for the storage of the data

Data should always be seen as an asset and should be treated with due care and attention. Data security implies storage in a system with appropriate identification codes and passwords and that the computer on which the data is placed is not vulnerable to theft.

Data may not be transferred outside the boundaries of the EEA unless the data is going to a country which has appropriate data protection legislation or where an exemption has been given. If a researcher intends to use a form of cloud computing, then as a matter of course he or she should inform the informant that their data may be sent across a national boundary.

This principle was established before the arrival of cloud computing. If a cloud-based computing system is in use there is actually no way of knowing where the data is being stored and whether it has traversed the boundaries of the EEA.

Organisations processing data such as this need to be registered with the Information Commissioner's Office. Universities will normally be registered with the Information Commissioner's Office.

6.3.5   People whose data is being held have a right of access to the data

In the academic research environment a request from an informant to review the data he or she has supplied is unusual. However if the informant has been presented with a transcript of an interview, for example, and wishes to have some aspect of it changed, the researcher is obliged to comply with this request. This is good research practice.

After such a request the informant might ask to be shown the transcript again. In terms of this legislation he or she has the right to see it. Of course even without the support of the law it would be unwise to refuse to show the amended transcript to the informant, as he or she has the right to withdraw from the research at any time and have his or her data completely removed from the research.

6.3.6   If there is factually incorrect data then the people about whom the data is being held have the right to have the data corrected.

This point has been incorporated into the above as these two points are highly coupled.

Mostly, the instructions supplied the application for the approval of an Ethics Protocol state that the researcher should certify that he or she is familiar with the University's research ethics guidelines and with the data protection legislation. It is for this reason that this chapter has been written. A close inspection of the Act and a reflection of the way that data is handled by researchers will point out that if the data is ano-nymised, as it will often be, the terms of the Act do not apply.

Anonymising the data can sometimes be as simple as removing the name of an informant from a questionnaire or having entered the data from the questionnaire and checking it, destroying the paper copy. But with regards to interviews this can be more difficult as the informant could be recognised from his or her opinions.

However in general it is not a burdensome matter to comply with the requirements of data protection legislation.

In fact, for most purposes normal courtesy and common sense will re-quire the researcher to conduct the research in such a way that the DPA will not have a great impact on the way that research is normally con-ducted in business and management studies.

Chapter 7

Cross culture, class and language research

Ethics is not definable, is not implementable, because it is not conscious; It involves not only our thinking, but also our feeling.

Valdemar W. Setzer Department of Computer Science
University of São Paulo, Brazil

7.1   Introduction

When research is conducted within a different ethnic group[48] to the researcher then it is important to develop a robust research strategy which will accommodate the cultural and language differences between the researcher and the informants. A cultural understanding requires a thorough appreciation of the other group's norms, values, mores and language. It is simply not adequate to translate the research instruments and the informants' responses and then claim that adequate accommodation has been made and that the research will have meaning. Much more than a simple translation is required. Some people argue that it is impossible to research across language and cultural differences. In reality it can be done but it is challenging. It is necessary to admit that a complete understanding of the other groups' cultural processes and values will not be acquired, but with appropriate preparation an adequate level of cultural appreciation may be achieved.

Groups of individuals from different ethnic sectors in society may be encountered everywhere as many organisations continue to embrace the principles of diversity. The researcher needs to be aware that the way Western individuals see a situation may differ from that of a southern Asian from the Sikh community or a Kenyan or someone from East Asia, such as China or Japan. The researcher needs to be mindful of potential

---

[48] The following comments could also apply to different social groups.

65

and real differences in views of what different actions mean to the informants. What is considered normal in a Western community might be offensive in other communities and vice versa.

On the other hand, ethnic differences should not be exaggerated as people of different ethnic groups in first or second world countries will sometimes have similar or even the same values, standards of living, education, literacy and general social understandings within the organisations which employ them. Here the issue for the researcher is to be sensitive to any potential misunderstandings and this is not necessarily easy.

7.2   Going abroad

When the researcher goes abroad the circumstances are different and these differences become especially important when the researcher works in developing countries.

It is important to appreciate that in the field of anthropology researchers used to spend several years living in a community learning its language and some of the customs before engaging in research with local people[49]. Today this is not always possible in the fast moving world of business and management research. Furthermore, in former times anthropologists were not constrained by the same ethical processes as so many researchers are today. Today's researchers when working in developing countries need to be cognoscente of and take appropriate action when researching among people of different values, customs, education, standards of living and literacy. The fact that different languages are involved is only one dimension of the differences between the researcher and the informant. In these circumstances the ethics rules or research governance takes on a special importance (Brown et al. 2004).

It is worth noting that virtually no training is offered to researchers with respect to dealing with people from developing countries, let alone to

---

[49] Even when long periods of time were spent with local people there was potential for misunderstanding. The works of both Bronisław Malinowski and Margret Mead are said to have problems related to the lack of sincerity with which the local people supplied information.
http://culture.polishsite.us/articles/art465fr.htm and
http://culture.polishsite.us/articles/art465fr.htm

understanding how an Ethics Protocol should work in these circumstances.

This Chapter addresses the processes involved in gaining approval from RECs and the criteria used to assess ethical integrity.

7.3   Formal guidance provided

There are some sources of guidance available. In the first place guidance given by the British Sociological Association (BSA) (2002) suggests that access to respondents should 'in some situations' be done through a gatekeeper. A gatekeeper can be a person or a group of people, who can help the researcher gain access to the respondents. In a sense this is obvious, as a researcher will need at minimum help to find informants. Having found possible informants using a gatekeeper/translator the issue of informed consent is still important and needs to be acquired 'whil[st] at the same time taking account of the gatekeepers' interest' (BSA 2002: 3-4). An open and mutual covenantal approach by the respondent and gatekeeper is important because the relationship between the gatekeeper and respondent continues long after the researcher has departed.

Further advice is available from the UK Parliamentary Office of Science and Technology (POST). Their advice on academic ethical issues is that "[e]ngaging the local community in research planning and monitoring can help to ensure informed consent is obtained in a culturally appropriate manner, as well as address other concerns. Ethical guidelines suggest this can be done through local leaders, Community Advisory Boards (CABs) or similar bodies, the appropriate route depending on the particular cultural context" (POST 2008: 4).

7.4   The gatekeeper

Both the ESRC and BSA guidelines note that harm may be difficult to predict but that a researcher should endeavour to determine any possible risks prior to the start of the investigation. The identification of any potential risk would have to be disclosed to all participants in order to gain informed consent. Particularly in a developing country context, a researcher may have no option but to work through a gatekeeper. As previously mentioned a gatekeeper can be a person or a group of people, who can help the researcher gain access to the respondents but more particularly in a situation where there is any doubt, the gatekeeper will be able to help ensure that the respondents *are* giving informed consent. The gatekeeper can be an organisation which works on an on-going basis with the group of respondents, a so called active gatekeeper. For example, it could be a non-governmental organisation (NGO) or a Charity. It is therefore important in the ethical disclosure process to fully inform the gatekeeper, as they will help in the process of informing the respondents. A passive gatekeeper may only help with access to the respondents and not be further involved in the process. In these circumstances the position of the gatekeeper is not so paramount.

The gatekeepers may also have concerns about the effect of the research upon the respondents. It is important to discuss such issues and incorporate them in the preparation of the application for approval prior to presenting them to the REC. In addition to giving the REC a fuller understanding of the research project it will also help the researcher develop a rapport and relationship of trust required for the final fieldwork. It is also suggested that the position of gatekeepers should be carefully assessed by the REC, when judging ethical issues because of the ongoing position the gatekeepers may hold in the lives of the respondents. These relationships should not be harmed[50] in any way by the research.

In this type of research where the researcher is in the natural environment of the respondents, there is an ethical requirement to endeavour to leave the context of the informants as undisturbed as possible[51]. Whilst this is more normally thought of as a concern in ethnographic research where for example a researcher visits a previously isolated tribe and may introduce other Westerners to these people, it also affects business research in developing countries. Therefore the business researcher, in considering the ethical principles to address in the Ethics Protocol, can usefully be informed by some ethnographic techniques. Based on the ethical principle of leaving the context undisturbed the

---

[50] Harm may be defined as any physical or psychological injury or damage caused wilfully or accidentally. Whether harm has been done or not may not be immediately obvious and therefore the researcher needs to be on his or her guard against causing any distress at any time.

[51] An exception to this rule would occur if the researchers were attempting to use an action research approach. This of course would be unusual in any cross-cultural study.

researcher will need to consider how to enter the environment without bringing their own value system and challenging the status quo. It is possibly naive to think that the researcher will have no effect at all, as any meeting between people can have some effect. The important issue is that the effect should not be one that could cause harm. A researcher needs to give careful consideration to this fact before the research commences and they need to address it in the Ethics Protocol (Oliver 2010).

7.5   Cultural and Religious Issues

Weiss (1992) reminds the Western researcher entering an Eastern country context *'you will be what people in the field choose to define you as and you have little control over this since you are entering their cultural totality - they are not entering yours.'* He suggests that to manage this it is important to exhibit integrity. This integrity will lead to trust which is both methodologically and ethically sound since people will talk to the researcher if they trust him or her. The amount of time spent with the respondents will determine the relationship and trust developed. The researcher's job may include recording and later analysing, but not passing judgement based on cultural differences. It is suggested therefore that the requirement for trust in a cross cultural context is not only an ethical requirement but also methodologically sound.

It is easy to identify countries, such as India, where religion is an issue to address, but it can affect research in areas of the UK as well. It can be accidentally forgotten that the world view of many people is affected by their religion. In many Islamic societies, as well as other religions such as Hinduism, Sikhism and Buddhism, a person's daily life, and philosophy of life, can be affected by their religious beliefs more than may be the case in a Judeo-Christian Western society. This inevitably affects the ethical perspectives of these societies. These beliefs can provide a collective identity in these societies which should be understood and accommodated in the research. For some informants these religious norms are intermingled with different culturally appropriate views on gender and ethnicity.

However, it is even more complex than suggested above. In developing countries where there are large gaps between rich and poor, there are sometimes different accepted norms across these economic divides as well. Therefore the researcher may need to have developed a specific understanding of the economic context of the research as well as a theoretical understanding of the cultural and religious issues. For example a female respondent from a large corporate bank working in Delhi will almost certainly have different socially accepted norms of behaviour than a female respondent from the same bank who works in a rural village branch of the same organisation. The researcher should ensure that when addressing the ethical issues of informing/briefing their respondents they do not generalise across these divides.

7.6   Are your respondents 'vulnerable'?

The term vulnerability refers to individuals who may not understand the implications of participating in the research and as a consequence of being an informant may suffer some harm. In the UK Children less than 18 years old are always considered vulnerable[52] as are individuals who have various disabilities, especially learning disabilities. Elderly people and those who are ill may also be vulnerable as are people who are in prison or who are refugees. Homeless people would also fall into this category.

There is some controversy about the boundaries of this concept. Some researchers argue that all informants are vulnerable. If an employee is interviewed and his or her boss does not approve of his or her views then the informant could place him or herself at some sort of disadvantage. Provided the informant was an adult and did not have any of the encumbrances mentioned above then it should be up to the informant to give a fair and mature account of the matter being researched in which he or she avoids giving offence to his or her boss.

Researchers have to consider whether the proposed participants understand the implications of being involved in the research. If the research includes respondents who could be considered vulnerable the REC will require that the issue of vulnerability is addressed. Just because the people may be from a lower socio-economic group it is equally important not to be condescending towards them and equate lack of education or economic status with lack of intelligence or competence. As an ethical situation, this can be a fine distinction. Whether it is because the

---

[52] This age will vary in different parts of the world.

respondent and the researcher have different first languages, or whether it is because of a low educational level of the respondent, it is important that the respondents understand the disclosure statements and the purpose of the research. This may be done through translation or interpreters who may suggest ways to simplify the language. However, it is important that the message is not diluted or lost.

7.7 Informed consent and language

RECs require sight of the Letter of Informed Consent. If the research is to be conducted abroad then this document needs to be translated and the REC needs to be satisfied that the translation is adequate.

There are several issues to consider here:

- Does the language being translated into have words that actually mean the same thing as is intended?
- Does the translation read exactly as it is intend to?
- Do the words used and translated have resonance with the respondents? i.e. do they know what is being talked about?
- Are the respondents literate and if so to what level? What effect will this have on their understanding?

When conducting research in anything other than the native tongue[53] the researcher is reliant on translations and an interpreter. But it can be difficult to know that what is being translated, or retold, is an accurate reflection of what was said. There are two main ethical areas to consider when examining these language issues. Firstly, whether the subject of the research is understood by the respondents and secondly that appropriate translation and interpretation is being used during interviews.

These concerns can be addressed using three methods. Firstly the researcher can spend time discussing the concepts in the interview schedules and consent forms with a local fieldworker. Ideally this is a person who understands communication issues for the type of respondents, such as if there are caste issues, educational / illiteracy factors.

The second approach to ensuring that the interview schedules and consent forms are fully understood is to have them translated from English

---

[53] The native tongue is generally considered to be the one a person grew up learning as a child and continued through the education years.

into the local language(s) by one translator and translated back to English by a different translator to ensure the words had not lost their meaning in translation (Warwick and Osherson, 1973: 30, Ercikan, 1998: 545). It is sensible to also ask the first fieldworker to assist in this process to ensure that the translated words are still at an appropriate level of understanding for the respondents.

Thirdly, an on-site interpreter should be chosen. This person should be someone who is thoroughly bilingual. It is preferable that the individual also has some knowledge of the field of research.

The process of gaining comparability of meanings in translation is greatly facilitated by the interpreter having not only 'a proficient understanding of a language' but also, an 'intimate' knowledge of the culture (Frey, 1970). Therefore another Western member of the research team may not always be appropriate.

Formal letters of consent to be included with the documentation for the REC may need to include English versions of the informed consent forms for the gatekeepers plus a version for the end respondent which conveys the same information but may have to be written in English appropriate to the educational level of the respondents. A translated version will also need to be supplied. An REC may also require to see the retranslated version to ensure that no meaning has been lost. The REC may also require the curriculum vitae for all translators and interpreters in order to be able to enquire into their competence. Only respondents who are literate will read these written documents. Illiterate respondents will need the information to be read to them and a gatekeeper may need to verify that the respondent understood the issues. The consent could in some instances be videoed. Alternatively the gatekeeper could sign that the respondents have understood everything in the consent forms. All of these factors will have to be thought through and included in a justification within the Ethics Protocol. The issue of videoing the consent has further ethical implications that will be addressed below.

7.8   Video, informed consent and privacy of data

Some specific issues with recording equipment usage and informed consent need to be addressed. According to the BSA (2002: 3):

> *Research participants should understand how far they will be af-*
> *forded anonymity and confidentiality and should be able to reject*
> *the use of data-gathering devices such as tape recorders and*
> *video cameras.*

Even where respondents have consented to photographs and videos, it could be argued that these forms of data are personal data, and therefore the ethical concerns should be fully addressed. As transcripts of interviews cannot be returned to illiterate respondents for verification, the use of video can be of assistance in ensuring that nothing has been recorded as data in interviews that the respondent is unhappy about, or they feel is too personal. The video or audio recordings enable the researcher to replay the interviews to the respondents at the time of the interview and any information they are unhappy with may be deleted immediately. There will always be the chance that a transcript will be subtly different from the video or audio recording. Allowing the respondent to view the video and make deletions is more responsible than not doing so, when the respondent is not able to read the transcript.

Where background videoing of buildings, offices, homes, workshops, etc., is taken, consent for use of the data has to be sought from the gatekeeper. If individuals are in these records, their consent should also be gained. Consent for the interviewing process does not automatically cover any general footage taken. This should be included separately in the consent forms. In the context of most business and management research the respondents will be aware of the implications of the use of video, however, if there is any doubt about this, caution on behalf of the researcher is required. 'Full disclosure' requires that the respondent understand *all* the issues, not just that the researcher has *revealed* them[54].

A further point for researchers in business and management to consider is raised by the Visual Sociology Study Group of the BSA (VSSG 2006: 4). They suggest that

---

[54] This applies equally to all research even when conducted in the home country. The researcher should not use acronyms, nor research or industry jargon etc. The researcher should be aiming for a low fog factor. The fog factor works out how many years education would be required to understand what is written.

[m]embers should note that in various cultures, certain visual research methods may offend the research setting and participants.

This can be more important to some indigenous cultures such as the native people of Australia referred to as the Aborigines. There are many countries (developed and developing) with indigenous communities and therefore it is suggested that this is another matter that should be addressed with the gatekeepers at the research design phase to ensure that they are covered in the ethics protocol.

Although video-based research is becoming more common (Aarsand and Forsberg, 2010) the ethical issues of how to present this data are still much debated and this should also be addressed in the research design and in the application for approval of an Ethics Protocol.

7.8.1 Disclosure

The ESRC guidelines state that a researcher should always conduct research which is of good quality and high integrity. They suggest that a researcher demonstrates integrity by ensuring that the

Researcher's control over results is made clear, specifically in relation to the ownership, publication and subsequent use of research data.

Whilst being illiterate or for that matter innumerate does not suggest unintelligent, the researcher should remember that, particularly in the developing country context, when talking about numbers, numeric scales, counts etc. it may be meaningless to an illiterate respondent. For example, a researcher may say that the data will only be kept for five years. If a respondent cannot count, five may be ten or one as far as they are concerned. Making this *meaningful* to the respondent can be challenging. Just disclosing the information is not sufficient – the researcher should ensure that the respondent understands the information. The researcher may be asked by the REC to demonstrate how they intend to guarantee this.

7.8.2 Using a leaflet

The formality of documents such as Letters of Informed Consent can be disconcerting in some geographical and political contexts. To help informants to understand what the research is about a leaflet could be produced including photographs of the researcher and interpreter. The leaflet is translated into the local language and given to the gatekeepers to share with the communities before the researcher visits. A leaflet may be less daunting than an official looking form. Providing this document enables the gatekeepers to discuss the issues with the respondents and for them to decide if they want to be involved at all. This leaflet can then be used again when the researcher interviews each respondent, who will hopefully recognize the researcher and recall many of the previously discussed issues as the interpreter reiterates them.

7.9   Confidentiality

The ESRC (2005) guidelines, quote from the UK DPA 1998. When collecting data from another country the researcher may potentially be in breach of the clauses relating to material being transferred outside of the European Economic Area (EEA). The researcher should consider, in these cases, whether to comply with the UK DPA or to comply with the legislation of the country where the data is being collected. In many circumstances, the UK Data Protection legislation is stricter than that of the country being researched, and therefore the UK laws are the most appropriate to follow for UK universities. The REC may require additional information concerning how the data is to be protected when the collection is undertaken overseas.

The respondents will also need to be informed that the translator and the onsite interpreter will see the data. These people should be bound by the same ethical constraints as have been agreed to with the participants. Signed documents to this effect should be included in the Ethics Protocol attachments for the REC.

Files that require translating may need to be sent over the internet but they should be transmitted digitally on an encrypted connection to and from the translator[55]. Some RECs will require details of the software to be used for this purpose.

---

[55] There are many examples of encryption software which is available to download from the internet such as www.truecrypt.org/, www.nchsoftware.com/encrypt/index.html, or data transition services where the data is encrypted and sent to the nominated recipient such as www.yousendit.com/.

7.10   Harm

The BSA Statement of Ethical Practice (2002: 4) states that researchers should *"anticipate, and guard against, consequences for research participants which can be predicted to be harmful"*. The ESRC guidelines (2005: 20) refer to risk and state that:

> *Risk is often defined by reference to the potential physical or psychological harm, discomfort or stress to human participants that a research project might generate. This is especially pertinent in the context of health-related research. But, in addition, social science raises a wider range of risks that needs to be considered by [Research Ethics Committees]. These include risk to a subject's personal social standing, privacy, personal values and beliefs, their links to family and the wider community, and their position within occupational settings, as well as the adverse effects of revealing information that relates to illegal, sexual or deviant behaviour. Research which carries no physical risk can be disruptive and damaging to research subjects either as individuals or as whole communities or categories of people, such as those with HIV infection.*

In the developing country context, the less physical forms of harm can be of greater concern. An issue is that of the apparent power difference between researcher and respondent. Respondents may be overwhelmed by the fact that a researcher from a university or institute is seeking input from them. From an ethical stance it is the researcher's responsibility to ensure that the respondents do not feel vulnerable or overwhelmed and intimidated by the researcher or the process. The perceived power of the researcher can make these respondents feel that they are in some sense being tested. In view of this the data collection instrument and the general dialogue between researcher and informant should not contain any inferences that suggest the informant's culture is in any way under review or that the researcher is allowing their value judgement to play a role.

To manage the power imbalance and the vulnerable status of the respondents, the researcher's skill at creating empathy rather than sympathy is also a crucial element for the prevention of harm. Sympathy, which is primarily an emotional response, can create a feeling of failure and should be avoided. Empathy on the other hand involves *"being able to take and understand the stance, position, feelings, experiences, and worldview of others"* (Patton, 2002: 52) whilst remaining non judgemental. This is also a crucial element of what is required for developing *verstehen* or understanding (Schwandt, 2000: 192) which can be methodologically helpful as well as ethically sound. As it is suggested that empathy is important, this raises the question of how can a REC prejudge the efficacy of researchers in achieving this understanding?.

7.11 Coercion – Reward for participation

The issues of deception and informed consent have a degree of overlap (Bryman, 2008). A key issue concerning deception is that *"There should be no coercion of research subjects to participate in the research."* (ESRC, 2005: 25). This draws attention to the issues of whether respondents (as a whole or as individual respondents) should be paid a fee or expenses for participation in the research. In a developing country context where respondents could be living at or below the poverty line, or in many Eastern European countries where earning levels are still low, the ethical considerations of paying participants is heightened. This issue should therefore be assessed at the research design phase and included for ethical consideration. Respondents may be losing income as they could be earning instead of participating in the research. Ezekiel, et al. (2005) suggest that *any* benefit could be an 'undue Inducement' made to a vulnerable person. POST (2008: 4) takes an alternate position, based on the views of researchers working in developing countries. They advise that *"it would be unethical not to meet the basic needs of those taking part in research"'*. Since RECs themselves may have their own views on this issue, it is worthwhile the researcher considering the experience of other researchers within the same university or institute. There is no clear cut single view on the correct ethical stance to take on this practice. It is suggested that the researcher should first approach each gatekeeper, to ask what the preferred approach is from their point of view. This should give the researcher extra justification for the approach they choose.

7.12 Summary and conclusion

This chapter has not covered all methodological issues of research in foreign and developing countries. The intent has been to identify those methodological issues which may raise questions with the REC and to give some suggestions for addressing them. RECs can be cautious when a researcher proposes to travel overseas, especially to a developing country or to conduct research in the UK with a particular demographic involving cross cultural work. It therefore behooves the researcher to ensure that they are well prepared and have investigated all possible ethical issues that arise from their research design.

Chapter 8

Ethics Committee Processes

"Machiavelli is reported to have commented that ethics is something that you do when you are alone. RECs are charged with ensuring that researchers no longer have that luxury"

Biggs 2010, 170

8.1   Introduction

It is prudent for researchers to thoroughly acquaint themselves with the processes applicable to the Committee reviewing their research when making their application for ethical approval. The processes which guide and determine the role and decision making of RECs can be based on influences and mandates not directly or at times obviously linked to their purpose. Although the work of these Committees is easily misunderstood, this chapter offers clarification and understanding of what is important to the Committees. It provides a brief overview of the major processes and considerations REC are bound by and which determine and influence their decision making and actions.

A succinct yet comprehensive overview of what applicants can generally anticipate of RECs' reviews has been described by Wainwright & Saunders (2004, 314)

> *Investigators must be able to justify the research on the grounds that there is a worthwhile question, to which we do not know the answer. They must be convinced that the question is capable of being answered, in ways that do not involve unacceptable danger to participants, and must create a design that makes appropriate use of methods such as randomization, blinding, placebo, takes into account availability of other treatments for the condition in question, is based on an adequate sample with power to detect significant differences in outcome, and so on. They then have to*

produce an explanation of the study and all its implications that is comprehensible to all likely participants. In doing this they should have in mind the probable age and mental status of participants, and the possible likelihood of involvement of participants from varied ethnic or cultural backgrounds. These questions will have scientific importance, as they will impact upon the homogeneity of the sample and the introduction of confounding variables. They will also be of ethical significance and will be the issues that a lead or main ethics committee will consider

8.2 What drives the REC process

Even though most universities now have RECs and related procedures, the important concepts and dynamics which drive their process and decision making is complex. Part of what appears to be difficult for Committee decision making is assessing the risk related to the research, which Calman (2003, 67) observes to be due to the fact that it is not possible to know what risks research faces.

By definition, carrying out research means that the outcome is not known and thus potential benefits and risks not known. If they were clear, the procedure, treatment, intervention, would be classified as good practice, not research, as the risks would have been already assessed. It is therefore difficult to assess the risks of taking part in a research project as much is unknown.

Whereas the *ESRC (2010)* endorses the concept of *"light touch reviews"* and ethical reviews which are *"proportionate to the potential risk"*, the same sense of judgement or proportionality does not seem to apply to research in the UK which requires ethical approval by NHS and University RECs. For example, any research which involves patients requires that both the University and the NHS RECs grant ethical approval.

8.2.1 Regulating research

Regulating research is a 20th century phenomenon, but only since 1970 have there been serious efforts in terms of law, codes of practice, guidelines and regulations (Nicolson 2003, 18). Until 1980 ethical regulation of health research was an informal process and it was not until the late 1990s that research ethics became increasingly formalized (Douglas

2007; Biggs 2010). The ethical regulation of research other than into health related topics is a 1990s issue.

Whereas in some countries RECs assess the legality as well as the ethics, RECs in the UK are explicitly instructed not to assess the legality, which is considered an advantage when the law is unclear. Whilst this may imply that RECs are to ignore legal judgements, Douglas (2007, 733), without referring to health or any other specific area of research, more constructively points out how the legality of research can be considered distinct from its ethics.

> .... though ethics and law may be closely intertwined, most of us think, that it makes sense to ask of a legal (or illegal) practice whether it is ethical (or unethical) and visa versa. But it must be distinguished from the less plausible view that the legality and ethics of research can be assessed independently of one another. This might be denied, for example, by those who believe there is a moral obligation to obey the law, and by those who believe that legal reasoning inevitably involves ethical reasoning.

To succinctly underscore Douglas' (2007) point, Saunders (2008) notes that "*unlawful activity may be unethical, lawful activity may be ethical but it is not just because they are lawful that they are ethical*". A contemporary example which attempts to illustrate the complexity of this statement is the recent and continuing Members of Parliament (MPs) expenses scandal in the UK in 2010. MPs not only wrote the rules governing their expenses but at times broke them without rebuke or impropriety, a few of which resulted in criminal charges and prison sentences. There was no sense that undermining the rules adopted by the House of Commons was unethical since the culture of entitlement which prevailed among MPs allowed for and were used to justify it. Even MPs following the rules written for and by them in itself poses an ethical dilemma, considering who stands to benefits from them. However, MPs not following their own rules or laws was clearly unethical. This example not only serves to underscore the vigilance and caution which is exercised in the ethical approval process but also the need for the researcher to thoroughly think through the implications and intersections between law and ethics which will invariably be present throughout the research process.

8.2.2   Ethics questions

There are many ways to approach ethics questions with the possibility of different outcomes without being able to decide which is superior. There is really no final moral authority to decide the best or most appropriate ethics choices and RECs would appear to have no special advantage here either[56]. The practical issues related to this in terms of researchers obtaining ethics approval for their research is offered by Biggs (2010) below.

> *However, on the whole the general principles of ethical review are fairly consistent. As a result university, social science, social care and private sector Type I RECs all tend to apply the same basic principles as are adopted by the long established NHS RECs. Within this, RECs conduct critical analysis balancing the needs of the researcher and society against the protection of the research participant to form an opinion as to the ethical acceptability of each proposal. However, in spite of the broad similarity of approach, RECs are still charged with producing inconsistent and sometimes eccentric outcomes. To some extent this is inevitable given the characteristics of ethical review and the principles and philosophies upon which it is founded. The formalities involved have been standardized with respect to procedure, but the nature of the process invites differences of opinion and interpretation amongst REC members and between different RECs. It is perhaps trite to state, therefore, that the nature of ethical review is such that differences of approach, opinion and sometimes outcome are to be expected (Biggs, 2010, 53-54).*

> *Furthermore, Dixon-Woods et al (2007, 800) have noted that RECs' ability to say what is ethical is not absolute.*

> *Our analysis thus suggests that it may be difficult to identify any particular characteristic of an application that makes it 'ethical' or 'unethical'; what determines whether an application is 'ethical' is whether a REC letter gives it a favourable opinion.*

---

[56] This view may well be disputed by several different groups of people, including those who feel that their religious beliefs point to an unambiguous course of action with regards to research and other matters.

Patients may be considered to be among the more or most vulnerable people in society and therefore in need of greater protection. However, what constitutes being vulnerable and when are participants vulnerable is not always clear. It is understandable therefore that when patients are involved at any level in research, the REC gives what may appear to be disproportionate scrutiny to the proposed research. This can be the case even when there is very little risk involved.

It is understandable and to be expected that RECs are considered to be careful in making decisions about vulnerable people taking part in research. It makes their decision making easier and provides protection to the Committees knowing that their decisions could be subject to procedural constraint or judicial review.

8.2.3   Legal and policy framework

Ashcroft & Parker (2003, 53-55) report that research which requires approval by the NHS Ethics Committee is subject to Governance Arrangements for RECs (GAFREC) issued by the Central Office for RECs (2001) in the Department of Health. The GAFREC notes that research conducted by students for educational reasons is to be considered according to *"the same ethical and operational standards"* as applied to other research. It also clarifies that research which only duplicates existing knowledge or is not adequate methodologically is unethical, that resources and proposed methods be appropriate and that completion of the research is within a reasonable time. Since the research in the case study in Chapter 9 was granted ethical approval by the NHS Ethics Committee as well as the University REC and by the Business School of the University in which it is being conducted, the research can be said to have complied with the GAFREC requirements. What these approvals imply is that the research intends to make a contribution to the body of knowledge, be done ethically, be methodologically appropriate and be completed in a timely fashion, thereby giving formal and public assurances that the research is credible.

However, it is this intention upon which the approvals are granted and it is the approvals which give formal and public assurances to that effect as well as that the research is credible.

8.2.4 Legal responsibilities

Kennedy & Bates (2003) suggest that the essence of the RECs responsibilities are legal and ethical. However, the constraints and limitations of the legal and policy framework which guide and influence REC decision making essentially set the legal requirements, and as a test of meeting these requirements, give prominence to the legal obligation of reasonableness in the decision making. Kennedy & Bates (2003,16-17) state,

> ..... *the law does not require the Committee member to get things right. Rather, as has been said, the obligation is to behave reasonably. Clearly, the expertise of the member may limit what he or she can do, but the law is likely to require that any reasonable member finding a matter on which he or she is unsure, should seek advice, (subject to the constraints of confidentiality), and may not simply remain in a state of ignorance.*

In addition Kennedy & Bates (2003, 17) point out that the REC is subject to judicial scrutiny.

> *As well the possibility of legal actions for negligence against Committee members, there is a further cluster of duties imposed on Research Ethics Committees, which might be subject of applications to the courts for judicial review, seeking to have the decision of the Committee declared invalid..*

8.2.5 Lack of case law

Although the NHS Ethics Committees may operate according to a statutory framework, there is no case law to help interpret or clarify their statutory and regulatory obligations or to know what circumstances may attract legal liability. However, failure to apply the statutory requirements may result in legal liability. Common law principles such as negligence and judicial review apply to NHS Ethics Committees as well as University RECs. Successfully making any claim will be difficult because the rigidity of the present legal structure for RECs has increased the potential for legal recourse for researchers and those participating in the research (Biggs, 2010, 55-56, 59, 62-63). Although informed consent is not required for anonymous data and questionnaires, there is no case law in the UK which will assist in determining what the level of information is required for fully informed consent (Biggs, 2010, 86, 89, 96).

Since confidentiality is a difficult area of law, ethical approval and meticulous adherence to the research guidelines does not mean that researchers will always be safe from legal challenge. Although RECs decisions will be taken into account by the courts, they will make their own determination with respect to the public interest. (Medical Research Council 2003, 377)

8.2.6 Indemnity

A University normally carries indemnity coverage for the research its REC approves. NHS Ethics Committees are protected by NHS indemnity insurance from being personally liable for paying compensation. In turn, RECs also need to see that researchers have an acceptable sponsor in place for the management and monitoring of the research as well as indemnity arrangements to compensate participants if need be (Biggs 2010, 65, 71).

However, Jeffs & Mayon-White (2003, 77) note that since NHS RECs are not legal entities its members are individually liable, which requires that they ensure they each are covered by NHS indemnity as recommended by NHS policy. This is supported by the Department of Health (2003, 248) which notes that the Health Authority should take financial responsibility for *"acts and omissions"* of REC members.

8.3   REC reviews and discretion

Biggs (2010,9) stresses that RECs need to have a good grasp of research design and methodology.

It is important that Ethics Committee members have a good grasp of research methodologies and their implications so that they can assess the potential risks, burdens and benefits of a research proposal. Ethics Committee members have an obligation to ensure that research participants are not exposed to unethical research. To do so, it may be necessary to ascertain that the research has the required rigour to achieve its stated aims to produce the results sought, otherwise the participants may be needlessly exposed to the risk of suffering harm. Consequently, determining that research is properly designed so as to be scientifically valid as well as ethically sound is regarded by many as a central part of

*the process of ethical review, although this remains controversial
...*

RECs take their responsibilities and or obligations to include a wide interpretation and reach subject wise in their quest to ensure they are satisfied with the scientific aspects of the research as well as the ethics. This may not always be seen by researchers to be in their or their research's best interest. In spite of this, guidance or advice from the REC can be constructive in preparing an application for ethical review or in responding to requests for subsequent documentation.

8.4 Appeals and legal challenges

Unfavourable REC decisions may be appealed but few are. Since provisional decisions provide researchers with guidance about what needs to done to gain a favourable decision, complying with it invariably is the prudent option. Disagreement with RECs would poses the risk of an unfavourable decision and delay (Dixon-Woods et al 2007, 799)

NHS REC decisions may be subjected to a legal challenge by a researcher whose research application was not granted a favourable decision. Judicial review could usually only be expected after other recourses had been exhausted (Biggs 2010, 73). Furthermore, considering Dixon-Woods et al's (2007,801) position, a successful challenge would be highly unlikely.

The most effective stance for the researcher to take is to comply with the requirements of the REC and if that is not possible, to abandon the project and find another one for which approval would be forthcoming.

8.5 Rejection of application

During a six month period in 2005, in the UK approximately 15% of first time reviews of applications by RECs were approved without amendments, 64% received a 'provisional' or 'conditional' decision which required further responses from the researcher and 6% received an 'unfavourable' decision, which meant the researcher could not proceed and that a new submission or an appeal could be launched or the application be withdrawn (Dixon-Woods et al 2007, 794).

8.6   Managing the process

Since the process for ethical approvals differ somewhat between REC jurisdictions, it is not appropriate to provide a highly prescriptive response with respect to obtaining ethical approval. However, some guidelines about how to constructively manage the process may be helpful, particularly with respect to managing the paper flow, timelines as well as engaging effectively with RECs

8.6.1   Time frames

Be attentive to the dates when the RECs meet. Although the RECs meet regularly and usually monthly to review applications, time slots on their agenda for a review are generally allocated on a first come first served basis. Missing a slot for a specific date could result in unnecessary delays.

8.6.2   Completing the application

Carefully scrutinize every detail on the application form, complete it precisely as requested and submit whatever additional documentation is requested. This is particularly so for the application form for NHS RECs, which is quite exacting in terms of content requested and the process to be followed. The form has explanatory notes directed at many of the questions as indicated by various icons throughout. It is not always self evident from only reading the questions what is required or what should be addressed. The application form is lengthy and may with attachments be 30 pages or more. It is accessible through the Integrated Research Application System (IRAS) at: https://www.myresearchproject.org.uk

8.6.3   Responding to REC requests

When responding to requests from NHS RECs about an application carefully think through these and ensure they are concise and complete. Reponses to the RECs should be timely so as to avoid any delays in their decisions.

8.6.4   In person meetings with REC

An opportunity is provided for researchers to appear in-person at RECs reviews. This is to allow the researcher to answer concerns or provide information as well as to gain a direct sense of what the RECs' concerns are. All of this may be useful for the researcher in dealing with any sub-sequent REC requests and responses or to assist the RECs in making and providing a decision more quickly. The in-person appearance also pro-vides the researcher an opportunity to ask the REC for clarification, the latter, needless to say, advisedly is undertaken with forethought and clear purpose. The REC can also be helpful in providing general guidance to researchers, particularly with respect to initial reviews of their appli-cations. Attendance by the researchers should also give them a much better appreciation of the process the REC undertakes in its review.

8.6.5   *Rapport with RECs*

Particularly useful are Dixon-Woods et al's (2007) observations on how to avoid difficulties between researchers and RECs and how to construc-tively deal with these.

> *In many cases of trouble between REC and an applicant, failure to agree a shared understanding of what makes for a good reason is at the heart of the trouble. In practice, if a REC deems some fea-ture of a proposal an ethical issue, it is a brave researcher who would dispute their authority to do so, or challenge their prescrip-tions, unless very sure of his or her ground (Dixon-Woods et al, 2007, 801).*

Chapter 9

Case Study: Two Ethics Committees

Change is one thing, progress is another. "Change" is scientific; "progress" is ethical; change is indubitable, whereas progress is a matter of controversy.

Bertrand Russell

9.1 Introduction

Ethical approval for research has all but become mandatory throughout academia, the health services and other professional bodies. The level or extent of approval required varies depending on the nature of the research being considered. Although the process for obtaining ethical approval and the content of the submissions by the researcher to the RECs varies across institutions or sectors, there is a commonality of form and purpose in these submissions. This is intended to protect the subjects participating in the research and the public in general and to exercise due diligence to that end.

The process is largely driven by the potential for harm to research participants as well as by a latent fear of potential legal liability for the institutions which approve the research or within whose jurisdiction it is being done.

This chapter deals with both University and NHS Ethics Committees.

We have chosen to include this case study, which is in the area of management and health care, to illustrate the challenges faced by researchers when working across disciplines. To indicate what is actually involved in obtaining ethics approval, a relatively simple piece of research involving both University and NHS RECs is reported here. The research question is *"Is trust patients have in the doctor patient relationship related to outcomes in patient care"*. The methodological framework is a quantitative survey of the perceptions of 300 patients of the relationship using a structured close ended questionnaire.

The case presented and referred throughout this chapter turned out to be much more complex than originally expected. It required more time and effort for the researcher and the University than most fellow applicants seeking ethical approval for their research in the field of management or administration. The purpose of presenting the case study is to inform the researcher of the issues through which he or she will have to navigate to obtain ethical approval. The case study will also provide some insight with respect to the priorities of RECs and thereby help to avoid or minimize some of the time consuming issues in the process.

9.2   Management and healthcare research

When management research overlaps or crosses over into other domains, particularly those of health care or medicine, the ethical approval process and the related decision making becomes a multi layered, complicated and prolonged set of activities, which may take several months to complete.

This research required permission to consider the doctor patient relationship from the patients' point of view. The research proposal requested that a number of GP surgeries in England ask their patients to fill in an anonymous questionnaire. The researcher proposed that a total of 300 patients, 30 from 10 surgeries, participate in the research and that the researcher visit these surgeries to explain the research to surgery staff.

9.3   The stages of the research approval process

It may be considered that the ethical approval process is a continuum which runs through the entire research process from beginning to end. There are normally two distinct steps in this process – the acceptance of the research proposal and the Ethics Protocol. It can be argued that the process begins with the development of the research proposal, in that if there were ethics issues at that stage these would be addressed by those monitoring and or approving the research proposal. Similarly the process engaged in by the RECs not only deals with ethics issues but also comments on and directs the researcher to address issues with respect to the methodology of the research[57]. These issues may be inseparable.

When patients were requested to complete the questionnaire the proposed research in the case study had gone through six stages of review, three of which were specifically for ethical approval.

Stage 1: Approval of a 70 page formal research proposal submitted on in 16th April 2010 to the University.

Stage 2: Ethical approval was granted by the Business School of the University through which the research was being supervised.

Stage 3: Formal application for ethical approved was submitted on 3 June 2010 to the University REC and was granted on 20th October 2010.

Stage 4: Formal application for ethical approval was submitted on 4 June 2010 to the NHS RECs and was granted on 4th November 2010.

Stage 5: Formal application to allow the research to take place was made to two Primary Care Trusts (PCTs) in England on 7 December 2010 and approval was granted on the 4th and 10th of January 2011. In order to apply for this approval it was necessary to have the above noted NHS REC approval.

Stage 6: Letters of invitation were sent to GP surgeries in the two PCTs during the week of 7 March and 9 May 2011.

Stage 7: A total of 300 patients, 30 patients in 10 GP surgeries, will be requested to complete an anonymous questionnaire and return it by post to the researcher. The permission of each surgery is required for their patients to complete the questionnaire.

Biggs (2010) reports that the *"vast majority"* of researchers conduct themselves ethically. In spite of this, the various steps and processes which the research proposal and the application for ethical review were subjected to by the University and the NHS Ethics Committees, served to ensure that the ethical considerations and merits of the research were externally considered.

---

[57] It is recognised that sometimes it is possible to separate these two issues.

9.4 Committee advice and guidance

In the initial contacts with the University and the NHS RECs, both offered helpful advice and guidance to the researcher with respect to the proposed research. This included the need to consider the following:

i. Participants

- the rights of research participants
- consent of participants
- giving would be participants time to consider whether to participate
- offering rewards as a means of appreciation for having participated

ii. Methodological considerations

- recruitment of research sites, the questionnaire design and administration,
- letter of invitation to surgeries
- patient information sheet and consent form
- data collection
- sampling and analysis

iii. Confidentiality and anonymity

- protection of information
- storage of data
- dissemination of results
- individuals who have to be omitted
  - those under age 18,
  - those with impaired capacity to consent within the meaning of the Mental Health Act 2005,
  - those with learning difficulties the surgery receptionist is aware of,
  - those who do not adequately understand verbal explanations or written information in English.

9.5   Committee requirements

Some of the REC's notable requirements with respect to the research in the case study were as follows:

i. The researcher was not to be present at the research sites to explain the research and assist patients in completing the questionnaire. The reason for this was that the researcher's presence might be construed as being a coercive influence as well as compromise patient anonymity.

ii. The request that questionnaires completed by patients whilst at the research site and sealed by them in self addressed envelopes, to be left with the research site to be placed in a prepaid courier bag provided by and to be forwarded to the researcher, was not approved. The reason was that the patient returning the completed questionnaire to the research site receptionist, to be put into the courier bag, would identify the patient to the receptionist as having completed the questionnaire and thereby betray the anonymity of the patient. Also placing the questionnaires in the bag would mean extra work for the receptionist.

iii. A £5 voucher provided to patients for completing the questionnaire was dropped from the research. It was considered to be *"condescending and could compromise anonymity"*.

iv. An overview of the research results could not be sent to the surgeries which their patients could request to see. The results were to be prepared in poster form to be posted in the surgery so individual patients did not have to ask to see them, supposedly because their interest in the results would suggest or indicate that they had completed the questionnaire thereby betraying their anonymity.

v. During the researcher's personal presence at a review of the application an issue was raised about the wording in the anonymous questionnaire to be used in the research as not being appropriate. The observation was made that there were words in the questionnaire which may not be understood or be familiar to an English audience.

9.6   Lessons learned

Since the research in the case study requested information from patients, the University policy required that it be reviewed by its own and the NHS RECs. If the questionnaires had not been directed at patients, only the Business School of the University in which the researcher is located would have needed to have reviewed and approved the application.

The front page of the Financial Times (18 May , 2011) reported that the majority of the population in England, i.e. 55 million, are patients of the NHS. In view of this a patient is as likely to be a member of the public as he or she is likely to be a patient. If members of the public would have been selected to participate in the research and given the questionnaire to complete, the NHS REC would not have been required to review and grant ethical approval for the research. Since it was decided to select patients rather than members of the public for the research, it has substantially prolonged the ethical review and research approval process.

Surveying members of the public would potentially be more labour intensive and expensive than requesting patients to complete questionnaires. To do the former the researcher proposed travelling to various parts of England such as the Northwest, Northeast, Midlands, Greater London area, Reading, Bristol and Swindon and request members of the public to complete questionnaires and obtain a representative sample of at least 300 respondents. It is estimated that this could be achieved over a few months.

The major lesson learned is not to underestimate the complexity and time required to obtain ethical approval. In this case study, when the application had to go beyond the Business School of the University to which the responsibility for it has been delegated and it involved the University and NHS RECs, the time increased from a matter of weeks to months. However, more important is to grasp the importance of the above noted issues and concerns which drive the process and the steps involved, e.g., the documentation required, when and to what purpose and standard, and the total time expected to obtain the approval. Although the availability of materials which give an analytical view of what drives RECs and ethical approval process are sparse, Biggs (2010) and Dixon-Woods et al, 2007 do provide useful insights and references for the researcher.

9.7 Conclusion

What is and what is not ethical can be difficult to conceptualize and understand. As a consequence, the literal practice of "ticking the boxes" has increasingly infused the process whereby RECs assess applications from researchers seeking ethical approval for their research. Dixon-Woods et al (2007, 801) contribute the effect of this as being of concern for researchers and RECs alike.

> *Part of the difficulty for researchers is, of course, that there is no recognized external epistemological standpoint against which to assess whether the REC decision is 'correct'. .... Nor does evidence that RECs have reviewed a similar proposal in the past and come to a different conclusion function as a 'precedent' .*

In the end, the research described in this Chapter was approved and the work began in timely way.

Chapter 10

Some problems

The generality of men are naturally apt to be swayed by fear rather than reverence, and to refrain from evil rather because of the punishment that it brings than because of its own foulness.

Aristotle, *Nicomachean Ethics,* bk. 10, ch. 9. (384–322 B.C.),

10.1 Introduction

There is no doubt that the whole issue of appropriate conduct of researchers is a challenge and this is especially true because, as mentioned before, ethics approval outside the medical faculty, is relatively new to universities. Researchers sometimes do not realise that there are ethics issues involved and that ethical behaviour is essential. Thus one of the recurring statements in universities' ethics documents is the need to make all researchers aware of the ethics issues.

When new researchers are unaware of the importance of these matters they can sometimes see the rules and guidelines as being another bureaucratic obstacle and thus a challenge that they can or even ought to circumvent.

10.2 Researcher misunderstandings

Some reactions to misguided understandings of the ethical issues include:

- Recently a researcher was heard to say, *"I have given an assurance that I will not mention the name of the organisation which supplied my informants but they are the biggest manufacturer of widgets this side of the Amazon!"* The researcher was reprimanded.
- Another researcher proclaimed that he would study the way that professional service organisations employ expert systems to improve their efficiency and effectiveness. He was a part time

student working for a large firm of professional service providers. When it was pointed out to him that other professional service providers would not be inclined to give him access to their data he declared that he would lie about his type of employer. The researcher was told that if he did anything like this his work would not be accepted for examination.

- A researcher was recently approached by a management consulting firm with the proposition that if he gave them access to his data he would be awarded a scholarship by the consultants. Fortunately as the scholarship was a large amount of money he sought advice from his supervisor and was told firmly that if he supplied the data he would be in breach of the university's code of conduct.

- Even when the commitment to confidentiality of the data is not being breeched there can be problems with funding. It recently came to light that a piece of research was being funded by a tobacco company[58] and that the informants were not being made aware of this fact. The researcher was told that she had to contact all the informants and advise them of this fact and to re-establish if they still wanted to contribute to the research.

10.3 Decisions handed down by RECs

Stories abound of how RECs have refused to approve Ethics Protocols and how additional data for inclusion in the application has been requested. There are examples of how a REC has required two, three or four resubmissions before they were adequately satisfied and allowed the research to proceed. The resubmissions were not because the researcher had not complied with the original request for more data but because the REC had further thoughts about the subject. It is not unreasonable to find a group of people such as a REC to have additional thoughts but the researcher concerned was convinced that the Committee was changing the goal posts on him. There are examples of research applications being simply rejected without giving the researcher much

---

[58] The sensitivity of researching for a tobacco company is a 1st and 2nd world issue and does not apply equally to all countries. In some cases research into tobacco could be perceived as an appropriate thing to do.

explanation of what the ethical concerns were and without allowing debate or the possibility to change the application[59].

Recently an application for approval was put forward where the researcher wished to use video taken in a public venue to explore patterns of movement of individual people. The video captured several hundred people over a period of 10 minutes. The people who had been videoed were entirely anonymous and there was no way of knowing who they were or how they could be contacted. Despite this the researcher was asked by the REC to acquire Letters of Informed Consent from the people in the video before proceeding with the research. This is equivalent to the application being rejected out of hand. But in effect the individuals' videos in this case had been anonymised and therefore this decision was at best simply misinformed.

Another application for approval involved the use of a corporate database. The database constituted sales records of some 20,000 historic and current clients. The database was owned by a commercial firm which sold electronic equipment to the retail market. The researcher had proposed the use of data mining techniques to see if there are any interesting patterns in the demand for the products which could be modelled. There was no question of access to any individual's records. This was to be an entirely statistical exercise using this data. The REC demanded that the researcher obtain Letters of Informed Consent from the 20,000 clients whose sales details were in the database. This corporate database issue is an interesting one as it is possible to construe this situation as being contrary to the DPA. This would be on the grounds that if the records in the database were such that the information obtained by the researcher could be attributed to living persons then the DPA would be breached. As it happens this was not the case. In most

---

[59] Applications may be changed and resubmitted. There is no theoretical maximum number of times an application may be submitted. However within the NHS regulations it is possible for a Research ethics committee which perceived little or no change in a rejected application with so-called improvements, to declare it's reapplication as vexatious and thus refuse to consider it again. An application for approval of an Ethics Protocol would have to be rejected three times before it could be considered vexatious.

incidences data mining research is performed on a subset of a database and as such the identity of those described by the record has been removed.

An application for approval went forward in which it was proposed that a sum of £5 be paid to individuals who completed the questionnaire and handed it back to an administrator. There was no question of the identity of the informant being revealed. The £5 was a token of gratitude on behalf of the researcher to recognise the inconvenience of the questionnaire taking 20 minutes to complete. The REC rejected this suggestion on the grounds that it brought a potential unsatisfactory bias into the research equation.

A senior manager of a large financial institution who was conducting research for a doctoral degree was told that individual Letters of Informed Consent were not adequate as he needed approval to collect data from the organisation itself. He was the Managing Director of the financial institution. It was not clear to whom he should apply for permission as he was the most senior corporate officer.

A Senior Officer in the Army applied for ethics approval to study aspects of leadership among the other officers and men in his brigade. He was told that a Letter of Informed Consent would not be adequate from the men and women he intended to interview. As the researcher was a senior officer he could not expect anyone of lesser rank to try to withhold consent. This is interesting for more than one reason. Firstly it is a REC decision which is almost exactly opposite to the one concerning the Managing Director of the financial institution. Secondly the REC was unable to provide a suggestion as to how this matter might be resolved.

10.4   Our system of research ethics approval

The question which these stories raise is, *Do we have an appropriate and a reliable system of ethics review?*

This question cannot be answered with a simple yes or no. In an important sense what we have currently is a start to the process of developing sound ethics policies which will eventually lead to higher standards and a better understanding of the ethics involved. This in turn should lead to better research results.

The current process of applying for research ethics approval has produced one major achievement. It has made researchers aware of the need to be conscious of ethics issues. There is no doubt that this was necessary and that the current approach has not only put ethics on the academics radar but has made it a central issue.

However there are several problems which have arisen and these include:

- It is not enough to have made researchers aware of the issues. They need to understand them in some depth. Few universities have made adequate training in ethics available. Researchers often have poorly informed views about ethics considerations. This may be where the issue of research maturity becomes relevant. As mentioned before, a degree of maturity is required in order to conduct research with an appropriate degree of integrity.
- This lack of informed understanding can also exist among members of faculty. This produces the unfortunate situation where sometimes faculty are not able to give the best advice to their students.
- Faculty members are sometimes co-opted or seconded to a REC with minimal concern for how much they know about ethics and ethical decisions. This leads to decisions which are not optimal and it also leads to inconsistent decisions which can be demotivating to researchers.
- Requests such as obtaining Letters of Informed Consent from 20,000 people have brought ridicule to RECs. Another university routinely asks for ten copies of the ethics approval application form to be submitted to the Committee. In an age of concern for the environment and with the facility of e-mail at the disposal of all the individuals concerned this could be construed as an unsatisfactory use of natural resources.
- Inconsistencies, especially those which appear to have changed the goal posts, have caused RECs and the application process to be regarded as a chore rather than something which can add value to the research.

Perhaps the whole process of application and review for the approval of an Ethics Protocol needs to be re-addressed. It is probably true that *"The current regulations were designed to protect people from unwittingly subjecting themselves to harmful scientific and medical experiments."* [60] Some would argue that not much of this is relevant in the world of business and management studies. Perhaps the approach to granting approval for an Ethics Protocol should look more carefully at the researchers in an attempt to establish their understanding of what integrity means and how they see the ethical challenges they might face. It would be useful to discuss with researchers how they will be able to minimise the risks involved and deliver quality research which will be recognised as having taken into account the concerns of all the stakeholders. No doubt this would be more time consuming than the current approach and many academics are time poor. But it could produce better research and a more satisfactory research process.

Of course it is understood that offering more information about ethics and research will not necessarily make researchers behave more ethically, but appropriate courses will ensure that if any ethics misconduct occurs it will not be as a result of simple ignorance of the university's rules.

---

[60] www.historians.org/perspectives/issues/2000/0009/0009vie1.cfm

Chapter 11

Advice to researchers

Ethics, like other branches of Philosophy, is a subject where very wide differences of opinion exist between competent authorities.

Ewing AC, Ethics, The Free Press, New York, 1965

11.1 Introduction

Ethics is an important issue and all researchers need to understand that a proper Ethics Protocol will not only be required by the university but will also improve their research. It will also afford protection to the researcher if anything goes wrong during the course of the research. Ethical consideration is not a one time event, but an issue throughout the entire duration of the research. To be truly ethical the researcher needs to approach the research with integrity and not just comply with the forms and documents which RECs require.

Outside the medical faculties Ethics Protocols are a relatively new idea and so it is inevitable that there will be some teething problems along the way to a comprehensive understanding of the issues by all Faculty members. Therefore there needs to be a level of goodwill between the researcher and the REC members.

It should be realised that nearly all research projects from undergraduate to doctorates will require an application to the REC to approve an Ethics Protocol. Other research conducted under the auspices of the university or business school will also need the same sort of approval. This will range from research conducted for the purposes of writing a paper to be published in a peer reviewed journal to research conducted for clients for the purposes of financial reward.

It is important to establish the point at which the research commences. Pre-research conversations with prospective informants and gatekeepers may take place without REC approval if they are not part of the main body of the research. These conversations are used to establish the scope of the research and the possibility of using certain locations and suitable informants who will participate in the research. An Ethics Protocol is normally not needed for this stage of the research.

Application for the approval of the Ethics Protocol should be made as early as possible as it may take time and it may be necessary to make a number of revised submissions.

It is useful to think of the ethics approval process in terms of a project consisting of four different sections or phases. This allows the researcher to cope with each of these phases one at a time and thereby successfully have his or her Ethics Protocol approved. These phases are:

1. Preparation;
2. Presentation;
3. Justification;
4. Flexibility.

11.2 Preparation

Preparation to submit an application for the approval of an Ethics Protocol should begin as soon as the research question has been established or settled and the researcher knows how the required data will be sought, managed and analysed. Of course there may be some ethical concerns embedded in the research question itself but this is relatively rare. Prepare for the submission by researching the exact requirements of the Faculty, School or Department. The preparation should attempt to pre-empt any suggested problems by thoroughly addressing all the issues required.

The university will have an application form which will outline in detail what is actually required. There is an example of these in Exhibit A. Every university will have a different application form, but the issues in all of them are quite similar. Many universities have these forms on its website.

Chapter 4 has discussed some of the detail involved in completing the application form.

Make sure that all the questions are answered. If the information to answer a particular question is not immediately at hand, it is important to spend the time and energy to research it. Discuss the application form with the supervisor and perhaps with the Director of Research of the School or Department. It is also useful to discuss the application process with other researchers who have recently been through the approval procedure.

If the meaning of a particular question is not clear, then make the necessary enquiries as to the actual requirements of the REC and also why the data is needed.

If approval is required from any organisations outside of the university apply to them as soon as possible. It can take quite a lot of time for these to come through and this can delay the start date of the actual research.

It can be useful to find out who are the members of the REC and to meet with them to discuss their attitude to the suggested research. When dealing with only a supervisor then it is important to clearly establish his or her views.

11.3   Presentation

It is important to remember not to submit an incomplete document. Assemble all the necessary supporting documents and summit the application and supporting documents as a package. Compile the documents in an easy to read and follow format.

RECs often meet at set dates which may be published on the university website. Make sure that the application pack is received in good time for the next meeting. Don't carelessly miss an opportunity to submit your application pack as it may have to be amended and resubmitted more than once. Remember that the research cannot commence until approval has been received.

11.4   Justification

It is important that the REC knows why certain decisions have been made. Justify any issues where there could be a difference in interpretation and provide details of how these situations will be treated. Do not assume that the REC will follow the argument or agree with it.

Thus, for example, if it is planned to use a questionnaire it is important to say why it is believed this is the proper way to collect the data required. If on the other hand personal interviews are preferred, then this also needs explaining. In these justifications there will often be an overlap between the ethics and the methodology. This interaction between ethics and the methodology is virtually inevitable so it is important for the researcher to have a sound justification for the decisions made in this respect. Justification may also be required as regards the management of the data, the analysis of it, its storage and its final deletion.

11.5   Flexibility

It is unlikely that the REC will agree with all aspects of the proposed Ethics Protocol. Normally some changes are requested. It is possible for the researcher to disagree with the REC and to appeal its decision and different universities will have different processes to facilitate this. However, it is a difficult and time consuming process and it should be avoided where possible. Provided that the suggested changes do not materially affect the nature of the research then it is usually better to be flexible and to comply with the requirements of the REC.

11.6   Conclusion

Ethics Protocols and RECs are here to stay. They perform an important function for the university and if anyone wishes to be involved in academic research, he or she has to come to terms with how these Committees work and how to present their application in order to obtain approval for their Ethics Protocol. It is essential that the ethics dimension of academic research should not be seen as a one-off form and document completion exercise.

Ethics awareness will lead to better research as the whole university becomes more familiar with what is actually involved.

Chapter 12

Some end notes

Ethics, like other branches of Philosophy, is a subject where very wide differences of opinion exist between competent authorities.

Ewing AC, Ethics, The Free Press, New York, 1965

12.1   Introduction

In general this book addresses a narrow set of issues related to how to obtain approval for an ethics protocol from a university ethics Committee. This subject is actually located within the wider field of research ethics. The book has also provided one example of the procedures involved when approval is required from a second ethics Committee such the NHS in the UK. When more than one ethics Committee is involved the procedures are more taxing.

The issues discussed here are those which appear on the application forms for Ethics Protocol approval at a number of universities. It should be mentioned that the book has kept to those issues. However there are several other important ethics issues which directly relate to the manner in which research is conducted and which generally do not appear on these application forms. These include intellectual property rights, plagiarism, outsourcing of work, relationships between the researcher and the supervisor and examiners to mention only a few.

12.2   Intellectual property rights

Although not an issue which occurs on a regular basis in business and management schools it is important for the researcher to establish the rules concerning intellectual property rights if there is any question of the research findings resulting in a new technique which might lead to a commercial opportunity. Different universities will have different policies and the researcher should consult the appropriate authorities in the university if it appears that this may become an issue.

There is also the question of acknowledgement of assistance or in the case of academic papers co-authorship. It is sound policy to acknowledge whoever has rendered any assistance and to credit co-authorship of resulting papers if a material amount of work has been done by any another person in preparing a paper for publication.

12.3 Plagiarism

Today plagiarism is an increasingly troubling issue especially as it is easy to access the work of others through the Internet. The scandal in Germany where a government minister was found not to have complied with the rules concerning referencing for his doctorate is the most recent high profile example of this problem. In addition to what might be called "traditional plagiarism" there are now numerous agencies advertising on the web which offer to write a paper or even a whole doctoral dissertation for a fee. Clearly anyone availing themselves of such a service is transgressing the rules of a university. It is therefore important to have nothing to do with any such organisations.

12.4 Outsourcing

It is possible for a researcher to obtain a certain amount of help with the research process. Data entry is one example, as is the transcription of interviews which have been recorded. If a transcriber is to be used then this fact should be made known during the approval application process. Some help could be acquired with initial library searches. But it would not be acceptable for a researcher to outsource a literature review. A researcher could have an assistant make appointments for interviews with informants, but it would not be appropriate for the researcher to have another person conduct the interviews for him or for her. Help with statistical analysis is acceptable, but the researcher needs to understand what the implications of the statistics are.

In general the routine work which the research requires may be to some extent outsourced, but this should not extend to the intellectual contribution, all of which needs to be the researcher's own work. An ethics issue can arise with regards to researchers having the final draft of their work edited by either a supervisor or by a professional editing firm. In both cases it is important that only light editing is performed. The work presented has to be written by the researcher. There are of course difficulties regarding the definition of light editing. This can become quite complex when a piece of research is written in a language other than the Mother Tongue of the researcher.

Furthermore, the editing process, which aims to only improve the expression of the researcher, may in fact, change the meaning of what has been said.

12.5   Relationships

The relationships between the researcher and the supervisor are central to the successful outcome of research degrees. However it is possible that the supervisor can provide more help than is appropriate. Some universities are required to specify how much editing a supervisor may do for a researcher and such rules should be complied with. There is also the question of the appointment of examiners. It is clear that an examiner should be objective about the work which has been presented and thus it is expected that if the examiner has had a personal or professional relationship with a degree candidate he or she should recuse themselves from the role of examiner.

12.6   Conclusion

The above comments are provided to indicate just how broad a scope there is to the subject of academic ethics. The issues mentioned in this Chapter are not directly addressed by the current approval application procedures. However, if there was any suggestion that inappropriate activities were taking place during the research the REC could investigate these matters, along with others which are outside of the scope of this book.

Perhaps one of the most important thoughts with which to end this book is that a proper attitude to ethics is not a one-off issue which has to be addressed at the outset of a research programme. Rather it is about acquiring and maintaining an approach to the whole research process from beginning to end which has the benefit of making the research better and protecting the researcher from possible unforeseen problems.

Some end notes

Reference list

Aarsand, P & Forsberg, L (2010) Producing children's corporeal privacy: Ethnographic video recording as material-discursive practice. *Qualitative Research,* 10, 249-268.

Ashcroft, R & Parker, M (2003) The ethical review of student research in the context of the governance arrangements for research ethics Committees. In: Eckstein, S (ed.) *Manual for Research Ethics Committees.* Cambridge, UK: Cambridge University Press.

Baker R B & McCullough L B (Eds) (2009) *The Cambridge world history of medical ethics.* Cambridge University Press, Cambridge.

Biggs, H (2010) *Healthcare research ethics and law: Regulation, review and responsibility.* London, UK: Routledge Cavendish.

British Sociological Association (2002) Statement of ethical practice.

Brown, N, Boulton, M, Lewis, G & Webster, A (2004) Social science research ethics in developing countries and contexts. *Working paper - ESRC Research Ethics Framework.* York, SATSU; Dept of Sociology, University of York; and School of Social Studies and Law, Oxford Brooks University.

Bryman, A (2008) *Social research methods,* Oxford, Oxford University Press.

Calman K (2003) Risk assessment for research participants. In: Eckstein, S (ed.) *Manual for Research Ethics Committees.* Cambridge, UK: Cambridge University Press.

Central Office for Research Ethics Committees (July 2001) 'Governance arrangements for NHS Research Ethics Committees', London, UK: Department of Health. Retrieved 9 March 2011 from: http://www.dh.gov.uk/en/Publicationsandstatistics/Publications/PubicationsLibrary/index.htm

Department of Health (2003) NHS indemnity - arrangements for clinical negligence claims in the NHS. In: Eckstein, S (ed.) *Manual for Research Ethics Committees.* Cambridge, UK: Cambridge University Press.

Dixon-Woods, M, Angell, E, Ashcroft, R E & Bryman, A (2007) 'Written work: The social functions of Research Ethics Committee letters', *Social Science and Medicine,* 65: 792-802.

Douglas, T M (2007) 'Ethics committees and the legality of research', *Journal of Medical Ethics,* 33:732-736.

Economic and Social Research Council (2010) 'Framework for Research Ethics(FRE)', Swindon, UK: Economic and Social Research Council. Retrieved 11 March 2011 from: http://www.esrc.ac.uk/about-src/information/research-ethics.aspx

Economics and Social Research Council (2005) Research ethics framework. Swindon, ESRC.

Ercikan, K (1998) Translation effects in international assessments. *International Journal of Educational Research,* 29, 543-553.

Ezekiel, J E, Currie, X E & Herman, A (2005) Undue inducement in clinical research in developing countries: Is it a worry? *The Lancet,* 366, 336-340.

Financial Times (18 May 2011) 'News Briefing', Financial Times, 1

Frey, F (1970) Cross-cultural survey research in political science. In Holt, R & Turner , J (Eds.) *The methodology of comparative research.* New York The Free Press

Human D and Fluss S S (2001) The World Medical Association's Declaration of Helsinki: Historical and Contemporary Perspectives, World Medical Association
http://www.wma.net/en/20activities/10ethics/10helsinki/draft_historical_c ontemporary_perspectives.pdf accessed 21/02/2011

Jeffs, J & Mayon-White, R Indemnity in medical research. In: Eckstein, S (ed.) *Manual for Research Ethics Committees.* Cambridge, UK: Cambridge University Press.

Kennedy, I & Bates, P (2003) Research ethics committee and the law. In: Eckstein, S (ed.) *Manual for Research Ethics Committees.* Cambridge, UK: Cambridge University Press.

Medical Research Council (2003) Personal information in medical research. In: Eckstein, S (ed.) *Manual for Research Ethics Committees.* Cambridge, UK: Cambridge University Press.

National Patient Safety Agency (2011) 'IRAS Integrated Research Application System', Version 3.1. Retrieved 2 June 2011 from
https://www.myresearchproject.org.uk

Nicholson, R H (2003) The regulation of medical research: a historical overview. In: Eckstein, S (ed.) *Manual for Research Ethics Committees.* Cambridge, UK: Cambridge University Press.

Oliver, P (2010) *The student's guide to research ethics,* Maidenhead, Open University Press.

Parliamentary Office Of Science And Technology (2008) Research ethics in developing countries. In Post (Ed.).

Patton, M Q (2002) *Qualitative research & evaluation methods,* Sage Publications Inc, Thousand Oaks CA.

Punch M (1996) *Dirty Business*, Sage Publications, Ltd, London.

Rothman D J (2003) *Strangers by the bedside. A history of how law and bioethics transformed medical decision making* AldineTransaction Piscataway, NJ,

Saunders J (2008) 'Research ethics committees & the law', Sheffield, UK: University of Sheffield. Retrieved 11 March 2011 from:
http://www.shef.ac.uk/ris/other/gov-ethics/researchethics/further-guidance/educationresources/humantissue.html

Schwandt, T A (2000) Three epistemological stances for qualitative inquiry: Interpretivism, Hermeneutics, and social constructivism. IN Denzin, N K & Lincoln, Y S (Eds.) *Handbook of qualitative research.* 2nd ed. Thousand Oaks CA, Sage.

Reference list

Schwenzer K J & Durbin C G (2004) The spectrum of respiratory care research: Prospective clinical research *Respiratory Care* 49, 10

Visual Sociology Study Group Of The British Sociological Association (2006) Statement of ethical practice for the British Sociological Association – Visual Sociology Group.

Wainwright P & Saunders J (2004) 'What are local issues? The problem of the local review of research', *Journal of Medical Ethics,* 30:313-317.

Warwick, D P & Osherson, S (1973) Comparative analysis in the social sciences. In Warwick, D P & Osherson, S (Eds.) *Comparative research methods: An overview.* Englewood Cliffs, NJ, Prentice-Hall.

Weis, L (1992) Reflections on the researcher in a multicultural environment. In grant, c. (Ed.) *Research and multicultural education: From the margins to the mainstream.* London, Falmer Press.

Whitehouse v Jordan [1981] 1 Weekly Law Reports 246. London, UK: Incorporated Council of law reporting for England and Wales.

World Medical Association (1964) Helsinki Declaration http://www.wma.net/en/30publications/10policies/b3/index.html accessed 21/02/2011

Websites

http://culture.polishsite.us/articles/art465fr.htm
http://culture.polishsite.us/articles/art465fr.htm
http://home.earthlink.net/~rlindbeck/fletcher.htm#Biography
http://members.iinet.net.au/~gduncan/massacres_pacific.html
http://news.bbc.co.uk/1/hi/1136723.stmhttp://ohsr.od.nih.gov/guidelines/nuremberg.html
http://www.bioedonline.org/news/news.cfm?art=1294
http://www.britsoc.co.uk/equality/Statement+Ethical+Practice.htm#_relhttp://www.dailymail.co.uk/news/article-22015/Spare-skin-sold-weapons-tests.html

Glossary

Action research: An approach to research where the researcher deliberately tries to change the activities or processes routinely conducted by the research participants and or their organisation.

Anonymisation: One of the principles of academic research is that data should not be directly connectable to individual informants. The process of ensuring that the data cannot reveal the identity of the informant who supplied it is called anonymisation. Questionnaires can be relatively easily anonymised by removing any aspect of it which can be traced back to the person who completed it. However it is sometimes much more difficult to anonymise the results of an interview as the person's identity is sometime apparent by the type of organisation in which he or she works as well as by his or her job description. Researchers are required to make their best efforts to anonymise data soon after it has been received.

Appeal process: If a researcher does not concur with the finding of an Ethics Committee he or she may request that the matter be reconsidered at an appeal.

Case study: An umbrella term which refers to the use of a group of research methods which are used to investigate a contemporary complex situation where the boundaries between the situation and its environs is not clear.

Code of ethics: A list of the behaviours which are expected as well as a list of the behaviours which are prohibited by the group subscribing to the code.

Data: A stimulus to any of the 5 senses which the researcher believes will help answer the research question. Data has to be distinguished from noise which is also a stimulus but which will not facilitate the answering of the research question.

Data Analysis: The phase in the research process where the data collected is considered, processed and tested / assessed for meaning in terms of a hypothesis, proposition, theory or the formulation of new theory.

Data Collection: The stage in the research where the data required for the research is obtained using a preselected protocol.

Data types: There are a variety of data types but for the purposes of this book only qualitative and quantitative data are considered.

Demographic type data: Data which describe the characteristics of re-search respondents such as age, gender, education, employment, postal code.

Dissertation: This word is often used synonymously with the word thesis to describe the documents which are submitted at the end of a research degree or as a component of a taught degree. For doctoral level re-search it is often many thousand words in length and describes the re-search and the finding.

Disciplinary process: If a researcher persists in ignoring the findings of an Ethics Committee then the university may take disciplinary action against the researcher.

Empiricism: An approach to research which relies on primary data. The basis of empiricism is that it is based on sensed perception. Thus the research needs to observe the phenomenon which is being studied. This observation can be through the eyes of others. An extreme empiricist would assert that particle physics cannot be competently studied as atomic particles cannot in the normal course of events be observed. Few people would take this extreme position as they would agree that the existence of atomic particles may be known though the results of ex-perimentation.

Ethics: A set of expected behaviours which are required if an individual is to work within or along with a group. Honesty, professionalism and care not to do harm to others are the hallmarks for a code of ethics.

Evidence based research: Research which is based on evidence; evi-dence being the basis which may support or reject a theory, hypothesis or assumption which the research is aiming to test or assess. Some fields using evidence based research today are management, medicine, health care, education, social work and counselling.

External funding: Funding of research by sources external to the university or organization or institution where the research is being conducted or carried out.

External sponsorship of research: Sponsorship or support of research by sources external to the organization or institution where it is being conducted or carried out.

Gatekeeper: A gatekeeper is an individual or an organisation that can make it easier or more difficult to obtain access to informants. Gatekeepers are crucial to academic research in business and management. They can reduce the time and effort required to obtain access or they can prevent a researcher from gaining access at all. In researching abroad and especially in countries for which English is not the first language gatekeeper management is a critical part of the research.

Guardian consent form: A form presented to the legal guardian of a minor or some other vulnerable person who cannot contract for themselves to state that permission is granted to the researcher for that person to be included in the research. The guardian consent form has to be signed by the guardian.

Harm: Someone or some organisation has been done harm if they are physically, intellectually, emotionally, financially, by reputation, or in some other way worse off than they were before the harm was done. Academic research in business and management studies may more likely put an individual or an organisation at risk of harm than direct or indirect harm being done by or to the researchers themselves.

Health and Safety: This term refers to the group or the regulations which are charged with ensuring that any risk associated with a given process or situation is minimised.

Informant: An individual who supplies a researcher with information which may contribute to answering the research question. See Respondent.

Integrity: A concept which is difficult to define but which involves acting in good faith; being honest with others and oneself; and not always seeking to maximise the short term benefits which may be available.

Interpretivism: An approach to research which does not rely heavily on numbers where the researcher attempts to study the situation through his or her own eyes and through the eyes of informants.

Mixed methods: An approach to academic research with employs aspects of both positivism and interpretivism.

Modernism: "*Modernism is associated with what has been called an 'up the mountain' theory of science, which proclaims that we know far more now than we ever did in the past, ... and getting better as time goes on*". page 246 in Brown, B, Crawford, P & Hicks, C (2003) *Evidence-Based Research: Dilemmas and Debates in Health Care. Maidenhead, Berkshire, UK: Open University Press*. Modernism rests on issues and concepts such as objectivity in science; our ability to reduce large problems to several small ones; our ability to be able to discern cause and effect; the principle of determinism etc. Modernism understands that the world of today has been created by the application of the scientific methods to the solution of technical and intellectual problems. Modernism commences with the Enlightenment and continues to be our primary approach to science and technology today.

Outsourcing: The use of outsiders to conduct some aspect of the research on behalf of the primary researcher.

Positivism: An approach to research which usually seeks to establish cause and effect relationships. Deduction and the use of numeric data is the most commonplace way in which positivism is practiced. Positivism underpins much of the research conducted today in business and management studies, although there is an increase in the role of interpretivism.

Post modernism: An approach to research which claims that there is no privileged way of understanding the world and no one way of conducting research. A post modernist questions the scientific method and asserts that it is only one of many ways of understanding the world. A post modernist would proclaim that there is a need to progress beyond modernism to a more sophisticated understanding of the world and how it works. There are numerous ways of understanding the term postmodernism.

Primary researcher: The individual who is responsible to the Ethics Committee for the conduct of the research. May also be referred to as the lead researcher.

Qualitative data: Aspects or dimensions which do not rely exclusively on numeric scores or evaluations. Qualitative data will usually be in the form of words and pictures. It could also involve sounds, tastes and vision. In as far as qualitative data is used to describe phenomena numbers in the form of tables and graphs may also constitute qualitative data.

Quantitative data: Numbers which represent the dimensions of a phenomena.

Questionnaire: A data collection instrument which contain a list of questions. The questions may be a collection of highly structured issues requiring a *tick the box type* reply or it may contain open ended questions in which the informant may supply his or her own comments.

Quorum: The number of members of a committee required to be present in order for the proceedings of the committee to be valid and binding.

Reporting research progress: Research progress is usually regularly reported on to the agency which sponsors it and / or the university within which the research is undertaken if different. Ethics Committees may also require progress reporting and notification of and approval of changes to the research. The NHS REC requires annual reporting on the progress of the research it has granted ethical approval and it must be informed of substantial amendments to the research.

Research participant: See Respondent below.

Respondent: The person or party taking part in the research who contributes information to the research. The word informant or research participant is also used to describe this person.

Response rate: The proportion of the sample which responds in such a way that their data is usable.

Responsibility: The researcher has overall responsibility for the research from the beginning to the end. Although the responsibilities of the supervisor of the researcher will vary depending on the organization or institution which is sponsoring the research, these will usually include mentoring and guidance and a quality assurance oversight of the research. The institution which sponsors the research will likely have responsibility for ensuring that it is legally protected and offer indemnification coverage for the research, its employees and the researcher.

Sample: A subset of the population in which the researcher is interested.

Sample frame: The list of possible elements of members from which a sample will be taken.

Sample types: There are many types of samples including random samples, convenience samples, theoretical samples to mention only three.

Sampling: The process of selecting an appropriate group for a research study.

Scholarly activity: An activity which is conducted in an erudite manner based on rigorous intellectual analysis and dedicated to high ethical standards and conduct.

Self-report: Self-report allows participants to describe their own experiences directly. Questionnaires and interviews are the main self report methods.

Sponsor: The entity, organisation or in some cases the individual which funds the research. In academic research the sponsor could be the Head of Department or Head of School who has agreed to be responsible for finding the necessary funding for the research.

Termination: When the research undertaken ceases it is considered to have been terminated. Reasons for this vary but it may include individual persons taking part in the research changing their mind about contributing to the research, finding themselves in a conflict of interest or sponsors of the research or Research Ethics Committees withdrawing their approval of the research.

Theoretical research: An approach to research which is conducted using secondary data and discourse among knowledgeable students, faculty or other individuals. Theoretical research does not employ primary data.

Thesis: In academe there are two distinct meanings to the word thesis. It is a scholarly report based on an original piece of research required for many post graduate university degrees (and undergraduate degrees) and for all doctoral degrees awarded by universities. The word thesis also refers to the new theory which is contained in such a report.

Useable sample: That part of the returned questionnaires which have been completed adequately to be regarded as useful data for the research.

University: An educational institution of higher learning offering formal learning opportunities and programs usually after secondary school completion and leading to the conferring of a degree.

Values: Values refer to that which is important, worthy or of concern in people's lives. These are implicitly or explicitly contained in the actual responses provided as well the context from which they come. The researchers' values are important in that they bring their own values to the research as well as supporting beliefs, attitudes, standards and skills which shape the research from the selection of the research topic to the write up of the results.

Definition of acronyms

BSA	British Sociological Association
CAB	Community Advisory Boards
DPA	Data Protection Act
EEA	European Economic Area
ESRC	Economics and Social Science Research Council
FDA	The Federal Drugs Administration
GP	General Practitioner
ICT	Information and Communications Technology
IRAS	Integrated Research Application System
IRB	Institutional Review Board
NGO	Non-Government Organisation
NHS	The National Health Services
NIH	The National Institute of Health
POST	Parliamentary Office of Science and Technology
REC	Research Ethics Committee
WMA	World Medical Association

Some useful websites and blogs

http://www.ethicsguidebook.ac.uk/

http://www.esrc.ac.uk/about-esrc/information/research-ethics.aspx

http://www.the-sra.org.uk/documents/pdfs/ethics03.pdf

http://students.shu.ac.uk/rightsrules/resethics1.html

http://www.nres.npsa.nhs.uk/

http://www.kcl.ac.uk/research/ethics/

http://www.bizjournals.com/buffalo/blog/morning_roundup/2011/06/suny-research-director-quits.html

http://www.bera.ac.uk/publications/guidelines/

http://www.who.int/ethics/research/en/

http://blog.ted.com/2011/03/24/you-need-to-engage-the-ethical-question-all-along-the-way-a-qa-with-paul-root-wolpe/

http://www.ted.com/talks/nick_bostrom_on_our_biggest_problems.html

http://www.ipo.gov.uk/

http://www.jisclegal.ac.uk/Portals/12/Documents/PDFs/IPROverview.pdf

http://www.visualsociology.org.uk/about/ethical_statement.php

http://www.britsoc.co.uk/equality/Statement+Ethical+Practice.htm

http://researchethicsblog.com/

http://ethicsportfolio.blogspot.com/

http://www.researchethics.ca/

http://researchethicsblog.com/2010/11/13/chinas-new-research-ethics-guidelines/

Appendix 1

Research Participants' Information Document

The purpose of this Document is to explain to potential research participants the nature of the research which is proposed and the role which
he or she is being invited to play in that research.

	Issue	Detail (the following is a fictitious example)
1	Name of researcher & contact details	Jamie Cassidy e-mail and telephone number
	Affiliation of researcher	School of Business Studies (Part-time) and The Hi-Tech Corporation
2	Title of Research Project	Cloud Computing, What is in it for us?
3	Purpose of the Study	The purpose of this research is to find out if Cloud Computing can advance the following: - In Business; to sell and supply products or services into the cloud and the considerations of business strategies and processes to do this - In IT; acquiring, and using IT/IS services provided by the cloud to do business – will it be good for ICT strategy, the IT Organisation, and the company as a whole? - In the Hi-Tech sector we operate in; can the sector overall benefit by supplying to, and/or using the services of the cloud?

4	*Description of the Study*	The research will take the form of Interviews (external participants) and Interviews & Questionnaires (internal participants).
5	*Duration of the Study*	30 months
6	*What is involved?*	Send participants an overview of the areas they will be asked questions on when partaking in the interview.
7	*Why you have been asked to participate?*	You have been asked to partake in this study due to your experience in conventional and Cloud Computing, and have worked in an environment where they have been used.
8	*What will happen to the information which will be given for the study?*	The information will be held in a confidential manner while the work is being collated. Following the successful completion of the project all material collected as a result of the interviews and questionnaires will be destroyed. Data will be traceable back to you until it is anonymised.
	Can you review the data after it has been written up by the researcher?	The data may be reviewed at any time before it is anonymised after which it will not be easy to identify which data came from whom.
9	*What will be done with the results of the study?*	The results of the interviews and questionnaires will be reported in the findings section of the research dissertation. This will be done in a completely anonymous manner.
10	*What are the possible disadvantages?*	I foresee no negative consequences for participants in this research.

11	*In what way will the study be beneficial and to whom?*	This study will provide a useful basis for companies to understand Cloud Computing (private, hybrid, or public) as an option for business initiatives, IT Service delivery (part or whole), and any associated application in the ICT sector. The study will investigate, conclude and recommend what's required (or not) to achieve this.
12	*Who has reviewed this Study to ensure that it complies with all the requirements and ethical standards of the university?*	The Ethics Committee of Trinity College Dublin have approved this research proposal and granted permission for this research.
13	*Can permission be withdrawn having previously being granted?*	Yes all contributors shall retain the right to have their contributions to the research withdrawn at any time. In addition the contributor has the right to refuse to answer any question asked during the interview. They may also ask to end the interview at any time.
14	*Can you refuse to answer any question?*	Yes. The contributor has the right to refuse to answer any question on either the questionnaire or as part of the interview and you may terminate the interview at any time.

Appendix 2

Letter of Informed Consent

I, <informant>, agree voluntarily to take part in the research project being conducted by Joe Blogs as part of the requirements for his Degree Research at <XYZ>. I have read the Research Participants' Information Document and I understand the contents thereof. Any questions which I have asked have been answered to my satisfaction.

I understand that the information which I will supply is confidential and that it will be anonymised and will only be used in the findings of the research. I agree that the data may be used both in a masters/doctoral dissertation and also in papers arising from this research which may be published in peer reviewed journals.

I understand that I do not have to answer all the questions which may be put to me. The information which I provide will be held securely until the research has been completed (published) after which it will be destroyed.

The information which I provide will not be used for any other purpose.

I understand that I am entitled to ask for a de-briefing session or a copy of the research at the end of the project.

I have been informed that I may withdraw from this study at any time and that any information which I have supplied will not be used and any records held relating to my contribution will be destroyed. I do realise that this is only possible before my data has been anonymised.

Informant

Date

Researcher

Date

Appendix 3

Letter of Consent to Record an Interview

I hereby give permission to have my interview with the researcher recorded for the purpose of facilitating the creation of a transcript of the interview for subsequent analysis.

I am assured that the recording will be erased as soon as the transcript has been created.

Informant

Date

Researcher

Date

Appendix 4

Letter of Consent for photographs or video

I hereby give permission to have my interview with the researcher videoed for the purpose of facilitating the creation of a transcript of the interview for subsequent analysis.

I am assured that the recording will be erased as soon as the transcript has been created.

Informant

Date

Researcher

Date

Exhibit A

Example of an application form for an Ethics Protocol

TRINITY COLLEGE DUBLIN

INFORMATION SHEET FOR PARTICIPANTS

This sheet should inform participants of the following, as appropriate to the study:

- The background context of the research explaining its relevance
- The procedures relevant to the participant within this particular study
- Declarations of conflicts of interest
- The voluntary nature of participation: the right to withdraw and to omit individual responses without penalty
- The expected duration of the participant's involvement
- Anticipated risks/benefits to the participant
- The provisions for debriefing after participation
- Preservation of participant and third-party anonymity in analysis, publication and presentation of resulting data and findings
- Cautions about inadvertent discovery of illicit activities
- Provision for verifying direct quotations and their contextual appropriateness

Of course, the information sheet for participants will vary with the study at hand. It should provide all information necessary for informed consent.

TRINITY COLLEGE DUBLIN
INFORMED CONSENT FORM

LEAD RESEARCHERS:

BACKGROUND OF RESEARCH: *(explain the background, context and relevance of the research)*

PROCEDURES OF THIS STUDY: *(explain what will happen in this particular study, including duration and risks to the participant)*

PUBLICATION: *(explain the intended publication and presentation venues for the research)*

Individual results will be aggregated anonymously and research reported on aggregate results.

DECLARATION:
- I am 18 years or older and am competent to provide consent.
- I have read, or had read to me, this consent form. I have had the opportunity to ask questions and all my questions have been answered to my satisfaction and understand the description of the research that is being provided to me.
- I agree that my data is used for scientific purposes and I have no objection that my data is published in scientific publications in a way that does not reveal my identity.
- I freely and voluntarily agree to be part of this research study, though without prejudice to my legal and ethical rights.
- I understand that I may refuse to answer any question and that I may withdraw at any time without penalty.
- I understand that my participation is fully anonymous and that no personal details about me will be recorded.
- *<If the research involves viewing materials via a computer monitor>* I understand that if I or anyone in my family has a history of epilepsy then I am proceeding at my own risk.
- I have received a copy of this agreement.

PARTICIPANT'S NAME:

PARTICIPANT'S SIGNATURE:

Date:

Statement of investigator's responsibility: I have explained the nature and purpose of this research study, the procedures to be undertaken and any risks that may be involved. I have offered to answer any questions and fully answered such questions. I believe that the participant understands my explanation and has freely given informed consent.

RESEARCHERS CONTACT DETAILS:

INVESTIGATOR'S SIGNATURE:

Date:

Exhibit A

Project Title: ....

Name of Lead Researcher (student in case of project work): ....

TCD E-mail: .... Contact Tel No.: ....

Course Name and Code (if applicable): ....

Estimated start date of survey/research: ....

I confirm that I will (where relevant):

- Familiarize myself with the Data Protection Act and guidelines http://www.tcd.ie/info_compliance/dp/legislation.php;
- Tell participants that any recordings, e.g. audio/video/photographs, will not be identifiable unless prior written permission has been given. I will obtain permission for specific reuse (in papers, talks, etc.)
- Provide participants with an information sheet (or web-page for web-based experiments) that describes the main procedures (a copy of the information sheet must be included with this application)
- Obtain informed consent for participation (a copy of the informed consent form must be included with this application)
- Should the research be observational, ask participants for their consent to be observed
- Tell participants that their participation is voluntary
- Tell participants that they may withdraw at any time and for any reason without penalty
- Give participants the option of omitting questions they do not wish to answer if a questionnaire is used
- Tell participants that their data will be treated with full confidentiality and that, if published, it will not be identified as theirs
- On request, debrief participants at the end of their participation (i.e. give them a brief explanation of the study)
- Verify that participants are 18 years or older and competent to supply consent.
- If the study involves participants viewing video displays then I will verify that they understand that if they or anyone in their family has a history of epilepsy then the participant is proceeding at their own risk
- Declare any potential conflict of interest to participants.
- Inform participants that in the extremely unlikely event that illicit activity is reported to me during the study I will be obliged to report it to appropriate authorities.

Signed: .... Date: ....
      Lead Researcher/student in case of project work

Please answer the following questions.		Yes/No
Has this research application or any application of a similar nature connected to this research project been refused ethical approval by another review committee of the College (or at the institutions of any collaborators)?		
Will your project involve photographing participants or electronic audio or video recordings?		
Will your project deliberately involve misleading participants in any way?		
Is there a risk of participants experiencing either physical or psychological distress or discomfort? If yes, give details on a separate sheet and state what you will tell them to do if they should experience any such problems (e.g. who they can contact for help).		
Does your study involve any of the following?	Children (under 18 years of age)	
	People with intellectual or communication difficulties	
	Patients	

School of Computer Science and Statistics
Research Ethical Application Form

Details of the Research Project Proposal must be submitted as a separate document to include the following information:

1. Title of project
2. Purpose of project including academic rationale
3. Brief description of methods and measurements to be used
4. Participants - recruitment methods, number, age, gender, exclusion/inclusion criteria, including statistical justification for numbers of participants
5. Debriefing arrangements
6. A clear concise statement of the ethical considerations raised by the project and how you intend to deal with them
7. Cite any relevant legislation relevant to the project with the method of compliance e.g. Data Protection Act etc.

Exhibit A

I confirm that the materials I have submitted provided a complete and accurate account of the research I propose to conduct in this context, including my assessment of the ethical ramifications.

Signed: ....   Date: ....
      Lead Researcher/student in case of project work

There is an obligation on the lead researcher to bring to the attention of the SCSS Research Ethics Committee any issues with ethical implications not clearly covered above.

Part D

If external ethical approval has been received, please complete below.

External ethical approval has been received and no further ethical approval is required from the School's Research Ethical Committee. I have attached a copy of the external ethical approval for the School's Research Unit.

Signed: ....   Date: ....
      Lead Researcher/student in case of project work

Completed application forms together with supporting documentation should be submitted electronically to research-ethics@scss.tcd.ie Please use TCD e-mail addresses only. When your application has been reviewed and approved by the Ethics committee hardcopies with original signatures should be submitted to the School of Computer Science & Statistics, Room F37, O'Reilly Institute, Trinity College, Dublin 2.

Application Check List

* The following documents are required with each application:

  1. SCSS Ethical Approval Form
  2. Participants Information Sheet
  3. Participants Consent Form
  4. Research Project Proposal
  5. Intended questionnaire/survey/interview protocol/screen shots/representative materials (as appropriate)

132

UNIVERSITY OF DUBLIN, TRINITY COLLEGE

Faculty of Engineering, Mathematics and Science

School of Computer Science and Statistics

RESEARCH ETHICS PROTOCOL

When is Ethical Approval Needed?
Ethical approval is required <u>before</u> any studies involving human subjects can commence. This requirement applies to studies to be undertaken by staff, postgraduate and undergraduate students. In the case of collaborative projects involving researchers from outside the School, ethical approval obtained from an external research ethics body may suffice – evidence of same must be submitted to the SCSS Research Ethics Committee prior to the commencement of the study (see procedures below). In the absence of such external approval, approval must be obtained as per this document.

Additional ethical approval may be required if the project involves or is funded by an external body, for example, studies under FP7 automatically require such approval.

For the purpose of this document a "study" may be understood to involve a potentially staged series of different experiments to be conducted over a period of time. If substantive changes are made to a study following receipt of ethical approval, this will constitute a new study for which further ethical approval must be obtained.

Procedure
Completed application forms together with supporting documentation should be submitted electronically to research-ethics@scss.tcd.ie Please use TCD e-mail addresses only. When your application has been reviewed and approved by the Ethics committee hardcopies with original signatures should be submitted to the School of Computer Science & Statistics, Room F37, O'Reilly Institute, Trinity College, Dublin 2.

The Committee will consider each application and normally provide a response within two weeks but not more than one month later. Applications that are considered not to have significant ethical implications may be evaluated by the Committee Chair without reference to the full Committee. Applications will otherwise be considered at a meeting of the SCSS Research Ethics Committee.

When approval has been obtained from an external research ethics committee, and School approval is not required, a copy of the external ethical approval must be submitted to the School's Research Unit, prior to commencement of study, for noting by the SCSS Research Ethics Committee.

Please note that in signing the approval form one is making a commitment to review the provisions of the Data Protection Act, like legislation and College Policy on Good Research Practice. Please ensure that your study conforms to the standards of anonymity preservation and data retention set in those documents. Those provisions suggest a default proscription against making digital or photographic recordings of participants. A study which requires such records must include in the research ethics approval application a justification and documentation of the methods by which the statutory provisions and research practise guidelines will be met.

Note: These procedures may be amended from time-to-time following recommendation by the SCSS Research Ethics Committee and with the approval of the SCSS Research Committee.

Before seeking ethical approval researchers should:
- identify actual and potential ethical issues that might arise;
- reflect on how these will be addressed; and
- formulate procedures to deal with all such issues.

During the research project researchers should:
- implement the ethical procedures;
- obtain continuous feedback from participants about ethical issues;
- periodically review the ethical strategy in the light of feedback received; and
- if required, update their ethical procedures.

Composition of the SCSS Research Ethics Committee
The Committee will consist of a Chairperson/Convenor appointed by the Director of Research and two other experts – a member of the School's academic staff and an external representative. The internal and external members will be selected from a panel approved by the Director of Research from time to time. Members will be selected on a case by case basis by the Chairperson subject to their availability. Researchers will be precluded from the Committee considering ethical approval for their study.

Research Ethics Protocol August 2010

Index